Book I - The Yield

By Joyce Willard Teal

Copyright © 2000
by
Joyce W. Teal

All rights reserved. No part of this book may be reproduced in any form, except for the inclusion of brief quotations in a review, without permission in writing from the author or publisher.

ISBN: 0-9660215-3-3
Library of Congress Control Number: 00-92841

Cover Photography Copyright © 2000 by Morris Press

Printed in the United States by:
Morris Publishing
3212 East Highway 30
Kearney, NE 68847
1-800-650-7888

Joyce Willard Teal

Autograph page for "The Yield"

For: _____

Inscription: *Best wishes now and ever!*

Joyce W. Teal
Author's Signature

_____
Today's Date

This is a gift?
❑ yes
❑ no

From:_____

The Yield

The Yield, Book I

Also by Joyce Willard Teal

Sister, It's Not Okay

The Point System

It's O.K. To Be Different

Joyce Willard Teal

Many thanks to my good friends

Mary P. Young

and

Kay Green.

I appreciate their enthusiastic support of this project

more than they can possibly know.

May God bless each of you richly!

For my cherished daughter

Geisel,

whom I pray

will never fall victim to

"The Yield,"

and for my wonderful son,

Rodney,

whom I pray will never victimize

those who love him,

or

those who will one day

come to love him,

because of an affinity for **"The Yield."**

Table of Contents

Prologue

Introduction

Chapter I 6

Sherl, Mary, and Frustration
Jan, John, and AIDS
Lynn and Missing Lucas

Chapter II 12

Yen, Ron, and HIV
Robert Sr., Robert Jr. and the Gang
May, Gerald, and the Affair

Chapter III 19

Dexter, Dawn, and Herpes
Carla, Roderick, and Denial
Jewel, Steven and the Double Life

Chapter IV 26

Sue and No-Commitment Phil
Amanda, Gloria, and Hubert-the-Trapped
Ruth, Josh, and Maybe Dexter

Chapter V 32

Ida and Disappearing Sidney
Wilber, Ester, and Daughter Queen
Sheena, Boyd, and Liz

Chapter VI 40

Erica, Sam, and his Need for Freedom
Eunice, and Eugene, the Weekend Alcoholic
Luther, Lacy, and Perfection

Chapter VII 52

Matthew, Mable, and Discontent
Tisha, Tomas, and Yvonne
Nikki, Shree, and Mike

Chapter VIII 63

Stewart Stealing
Lauren, Luis, and Dr. Pat
Megan, Randy, and Gretel

Chapter IX 80

Donna, Neil, and Mannin
Gina, Alvin, and Infidelity
Renee, Earl, and Juanita
Asa and Darryll

Prologue

Although this is a nonfiction writing, names and places have been fictionalized to protect the privacy of the real people to whom these experiences belong. I offer my thanks to these courageous people for their willingness to share their private lives with me.

These people have suffered intense pain; many of them are still hurting. For their pain, for their bravery, for their willingness to share these experiences, it is my hope that many others will be able to avoid the pitfalls and ensuing devastation.

The children who are products of these relationships have been wronged. Many of them are filled with anger, the source of which they are too immature to pinpoint. Nevertheless, the pain and confusion which they feel is very real.

But make no mistake about it. Immaturity, for most of them, is a temporary state of being. They will one day, independently, fathom the source of their inner rage. Some will confront their irresponsible fathers; others will continue to smother and/or mask their resentment.

It is my hope by writing this book that the women and children who have suffered because of the Black men whom they have loved will come to understand that they are not to blame; they are victims!

Finally, there are two ways to read this book: the traditional way, from beginning to end following the sequence of pages in numerical order, or you may prefer to move between the scenarios, reading the initial scenario in Book I, and then reading its corresponding resolution in Book II. However you choose to read it, *do read it!*

Introduction

It is obvious that some Black men do not understand that their behavior is like that of white slave masters whom they claim they would have despised. They persist in behavior they know is wrong and destructive because of what it yields to them. One has to wonder if they understand how that behavior undermines everything else good which they may do. Just as slave masters provided food, shelter, occasional gifts, etc. for their slaves and it meant little, so the good things these Black men do mean little in light of the behavior in which they persist.

"I have to live my life," one Black man responded when confronted by his wife with an aspect of his immoral behavior. Now while no one can deny that this is true of everyone, exactly what does the Black man mean by this? Does he mean if he behaves morally, he won't be living his life? Does he mean that showing the maturity to make needed sacrifices that will keep his family intact will mean that he will not be living his life? Maybe he means that a lack of variety of sex partners some how robs him of living his life. Possibly he means that one woman, one wife, one lifetime commitment would rob him of living his life. Perhaps he means that expecting him to be a role model his children can depend on during their childhood and can emulate in their adulthood would keep him from living his life.

It's anybody's guess what the Black man means when he says, "I have to my life." I *can only guess*. But I don't have to conjecture about what his behavior yields. It yields broken lives. It yields angry sons with invisible chips on their shoulders. It yields bitter wives and mothers who are so troubled with the constant disrespect these men, who once claimed to love them foster upon them that they are not free to focus on loving and rearing their difficult and hostile children. It yields children who are so anger-filled and confused that they are not able to concentrate on learning while at school. It yields an inordinate number of Black boys and girls in special education classes who actually have average, and many even above-average intelligence. It yields improperly socialized or unsocialized children who very obviously don't fit in with children who have been properly socialized. As these children reach adulthood, it yields a repeated cycle of behavior which emulates what these children saw and experienced during their formative years. And so the cycle continues. Some Black men, it seems, are doing what decades of slavery was unable to do: ***destroy the Black race.*** Of course these men will argue to the contrary because they are in denial.

One Black man with whom I spoke at length expressed the following opinion, with no reticence whatsoever: "My children are grown, now I'm free to live my life." When I asked him to elaborate, listening carefully to him, I got the distinct impression that he felt no obligation, whatsoever, to cherish his wife, the mother of those adult children; no obligation to provide those grown-up children with the peace of mind that comes with knowing that their mother is secure and happy and fulfilled within her own life; no obligation to provide a role model for those adult children to emulate.

Another Black man I know is loved dearly by his family. His children, nieces and nephews idolize him; they know only positive things about him. They know nothing of his constant infidelities. They know nothing of his ongoing disrespect of his wife. They know nothing of his wife's efforts to keep his image untarnished in their minds because, as she puts it, "I know how important it is for young people to have a strong, male role model in their lives."

"Think of your family, think of our mutual friends. Consider all of the people who believe in you, who know you only as a loving, caring family man," one wife said to her husband, a Black man, in an effort to convince him to abandon his immoral behavior. She shared with me that his only response was, "I have to do what I have to do."

How revealing. What this says, in essence, is that his family, their mutual friends, all of the people who believe in him, are secondary to *his yield.* It is the one element to which priority is given. What *he* wants to do is all that matters. It tops *his* list. It's as if he is a seven-year-old child who insists on his own way, regardless of how illogical that way may be or who may be damaged or hurt by his behavior. He is in denial; consequently, the fact that his behavior is wreaking havoc in the lives of people who love and depend upon him bears no significance for him. *That's their problem,* is his obvious sentiment.

One Black man reportedly leaves home around five-thirty in the morning, a Saturday morning. He says he's meeting some guys at a local gym to play basketball. His family neither sees him nor hears from him for several days. He returns with no explanation or apology. He refuses to look, so he doesn't see the pain and devastation in his family's eyes. He goes on about his life as if all is well, nothing is wrong. Another illustration of his *denial.*

The young son in his home is old enough to sense that something is amiss. He knows that Dad doesn't work on Saturday and that he has chosen to spend his day elsewhere. He's not yet old enough to verbalize these thoughts, nor even to formulate them clearly, but he is old enough to feel rejection; he feels unworthy of his father's free time. He feels angry, but he doesn't understand why, or who the target of his anger should be. He is becoming an unguided missile seeking a target. He does not understand that the topography of childhood should not be rough terrain, that the conflicting thoughts and feelings which he is experiencing should not be a part of his young life. But fathers such as his do nothing to make this terrain gentle, and rolling, and easily negotiable.

On Monday when he goes to school, he listens during *show and tell* while others talk excitedly about the great times they spent with their moms and dads during the weekend. He listens attentively for several minutes, then he causes a disruption. Teacher responds, "John, I have told you that it is rude to interrupt while someone else is speaking." John ignores her and continues his disruptive behavior. Teacher asks her assistant to take John to the office for a conference with one of the counselors. One scenario, repeated thousands of times throughout the United States. Teacher wonders why John is disruptive, uncooperative, and unresponsive. *Teacher is clueless.* She knows nothing of the rejection John is beginning to feel. She has no idea that John is trying to drown out the drumbeats of *Dad! Dad! Dad!* that are reverberating and echoing inside his brain, inside his heart. Teacher knows only that something is missing in John's socialization.

The Yield

by

Joyce Willard Teal

Chapter I

Sherl, Mary, and Frustration

Mary is just over an hour late getting home. Her mom has told her to be home by midnight. At 1 a.m., Sherl is frantic. She wonders not only *where Mary is*, but *where Mary's dad, her husband of seventeen years is also*. She desperately needs to share her concern for Mary with him. Sherl has begun to suspect that Mary has gotten involved in premarital sex, and with all she hears about teens and drugs in the news these days, she fears maybe even drugs.

Mary is seeking the close, male companionship which is now missing between herself and her dad. He once doted on Mary, giving her piggyback rides, carrying her around on his shoulders, tossing her high into the air, delighting in her squeals of joy. He might've forgotten all about that, *but Mary hasn't*. She takes his disinterest now as rejection, even though she's shared these feelings with no one. She is hoping, maybe even subconsciously, *that her behavior will get his attention.*

By 2 a.m. Sherl is even more frantic, imagining *a terrible accident* or God knows what else. Mary isn't home yet and she hasn't called either. Sherl is contemplating calling the police when she hears a car stop outside. She pulls the curtain aside to get a closer look. The car has pulled into their driveway. Sherl opens the door as simultaneously Mary gets out of the car.

"Exactly what time did I tell you to be home, Young Lady!" Sherl screams. She feels so frustrated, as if she is losing control. She knows that Mary's father would probably be able to handle this situation with Mary much better. The two of them had been so close, but he is hardly ever home now. She can't remember the last time she has seen the two of them with their heads together like they used to do all the time. She'd often teased them about plotting mischief. Fleetingly, she thinks that Mary can't help but miss those times. She resolves to speak with him about spending more time with Mary. But right now she has to handle this situation alone.

Another frustrated mother, another angry, rebellious daughter. Was *the yield worth it?*

Jan, John, and AIDS

Jan has just been informed that she tested positive for the AIDS virus. At first she is disbelieving. "How can this be?" she asks the doctor. "I've been married for fourteen years and have never been unfaithful to my husband."

Regretfully the doctor informs her that her husband could be the source of her infection. "No way!" she screams. "John would never risk the children's health, or mine!"

The doctor, Dr. Potts, advises Jan to get the children, Evette and Evelyn tested as soon as possible. "It's unlikely that either of them has been infected," he says consolingly. "But you'll feel better knowing that. John should also be tested immediately."

Jan takes the children in for tests. Their constant questions about why they have to take a blood test grate on her already jangling nerves. She answers them as best she can without telling them the real reason. *There's no reason why I should burden them with this unless I have to,* she says to herself.

Days pass. John is on a business trip, has been gone for most of the week and will be home on Friday, which is now the following day. Jan has learned that both the children are negative and has breathed a sigh of relief. *Thank you, God,* she keeps repeating to herself.

Jan has not spoken with John since she learned of her predicament because he hasn't called and she doesn't have a number where she can reach him.

Sometimes when he travels, he has to spend the night is different hotels in different cities, so she doesn't always have a number where he can be reached. Once he was conscientious about making sure he called regularly to check on her and the girls when he was out of the city, but he's become increasingly neglectful of this duty, of late.

She's been debating with herself as to whether or not to tell him on the phone if he does call. *I want to look into his eyes when I tell him. I need to see his reaction when he learns what he has done to us,* she says to herself. Jan feels the need to watch his reaction as this information is revealed to him. Was *the yield* worth it?

Lynn and Missing Lucas

Lynn and Lucas have been married for nineteen years. They have three children. Their eldest, Anne, is sixteen, and she has been a *Daddy's girl* since birth. But for the past three years, *Daddy* has spent increasingly less time at home. Anne misses their times together. She has now been dating Todd for about a year. Lately they have been spending more and more time together and have become intimate. Anne has just confessed to her mother that she has missed her period for the past two months. Lynn thinks immediately of the times when she has said to Lucas, "You're neglecting the children and me. We hardly see you anymore; we all miss you." Lucas always makes excuses: "I have to work; it's up to me to earn a living. What do you want from me?"

But Lucas is not spending all of his time away from home earning a living for his family. For about three years now he has been involved in a relationship with Beth, a professional woman, who is fifteen years his junior. Beth believes that Lucas is a divorced man who will soon ask her to become his wife, *as soon as he gets a few things straight.* She is in love with him and looks forward to their times together. His family loves him too and also anticipates the times when he has leisure time and can be with them. Anne especially feels the loss. She always felt so close to him, that she was special to him. *And she is,* but Lucas has not allowed his love for Anne to interfere with his ongoing conquests. One has to wonder if Anne's new-found closeness with Todd is a substitute for her *missing father. The yield,* is it worth it?

Chapter II

Ron, Yen, and HIV

Yen is six-and-a-half months pregnant. She, and quite possibly her unborn child, are HIV positive. Yen's husband of six years has admitted to being unfaithful to her. "It just happened," Ron says. "Only once. You were visiting your mother in Omaha and I was lonely. I'd had a few beers and I guess I was vulnerable. I'm sorry."

Ron is indeed sorry, and not just in the way he means. Rain just happens, and it wasn't even cloudy when the picnic started. Milk just happens to spill, and one can't even account for how or why the glass fell. Hail just happens, and the temperature isn't even below freezing. Affairs don't just happen. People make conscious decisions to have, *or not to have sex*, all the time. When people have sex, in overwhelming majority of instances, it is a conscious choice that they make.

The Black man, like every other normal adult, is responsible for his own behavior, for his own choices. *His behavior is not something that just happens to him.* Giving in to some woman, sometimes even a strange one about whom he knows nothing, just to keep her from thinking of him as weak or homosexual, or something less than a man in her opinion, says to his family that he doesn't value *their* opinion of him. It says that their estimation of his character doesn't count. It says that what some *strange* woman thinks about him is more important to him than the opinion his family holds. *The yield*, is it worth it?

Robert Sr., Robert Jr., and the Gang

Robert Jr. (Bobby), has always resisted joining a gang, although there are plenty of gangs at his high school. He has a nice group of friends and has always done well in school. Four months ago his father told him, "Your mother and I don't love each other anymore. We won't be living together after today. You'll live here with your mother, but you can visit me any time you want. I'll also visit you often. We'll see one another as much as when we were living here together."

But Robert Sr. lied. He is already in a serious relationship with a woman who knows, by virtue of the fact that they work for the same agency, that Robert's salary is in excess of a hundred thousand dollars a year. She has bragged to her friends, "I'm gonna get him, no matter what it takes!" She neither knows nor cares that June and Robert married as college sophomores; that June *dropped out* to support Robert so that he could complete his education.

June continued to work for several years into the marriage. She and Robert didn't mind the struggle together. They had a good marriage, and when Bobby was born, both were ecstatic. Robert agreed that June should quit her job and stay home with the baby. Nothing was too good for their son. The family was closeknit and content. They loved one another and enjoyed being together.

As the years passed, the family thrived. Robert received repeated job promotions. Bobby, a good student, made exceptional grades. He was always receiving one award or another at school. June was a contented wife and mother, *taking good care of both my handsome men,* as she frequently referred to Bobby and his dad.

But Robert's eye has begun to rove. He no longer rushes home from work. He no longer takes off for parent conferences or to accompany Bobby's class on an occasional field trip. June and Bobby hear more and more excuses concerning why Robert cannot, or will not be home directly after work. Bobby's grades began to drop. Now he feels angry all the time. He begins to get into trouble at school, something he has never done heretofore. The nice boys with whom he had previously associated begin to avoid him. To show his *old friends* that he doesn't care about their refusal to include him in their plans, Bobby joins a gang.

Bobby's new friends tell him that he has to commit a crime before he can be considered an official member of the gang. That night Bobby and his new friends go to the local mall. Bobby goes into the Men's Department of a large store in the mall. He takes two expensive sweaters into a dressing room. He puts one of the sweaters on, then he puts his shirt back on over the sweater. He heads for the exit.

Bobby walks slowly, feigning casualness, back to the table from which he has taken the two sweaters. He puts one of the sweaters back on the table. He heads for the exit. As soon as he exits the store, a store detective who has been watching Bobby the entire time approaches him and demands his return to the store. He takes Bobby into the store manager's office and asks him to have a seat; he tells him to wait. "You took two sweaters into the dressing room, but you returned only one of the sweaters to the table," the detective says. "Where's the other sweater?" Police are summoned.

Bobby's mother, June, is called; she is distraught. She tries to reach Robert Sr. but is told that he has called in sick. He is, in fact, spending the day with his new love interest. She has also called in sick.

Robert's wife and son need him, but he is inaccessible to them. Bobby is confused and unhappy about his father's seemingly sudden disinterest. Now he is in trouble with the law. *The yield,* was it worth it?

May, Gerald, and the Affair

May and Gerald were married their senior year of college. They had intended to wait for graduation, but when May discovered that she was pregnant, they both agreed that it didn't make sense to wait. After all, they loved each other. They had been dating since high school. Their twins, Laura and Sarah were born two months after they graduated from college.

Life is good for the Hemsteads. They are in love. Their twins are beautiful and thriving. They both have landed good, professional jobs. They alternate picking the twins up from May's mother who keeps them while they work.

Occasionally Gerald will call May at work on his day to pick the twins up to say that he is going to be unavoidably delayed, that he has to work late, and to ask her to pick them up. May always agrees. She doesn't mind at all. She misses them all day and can hardly wait to see them at each day's end.

On one such day, May has agreed to pick the twins up, but on her way out of the door she remembers that this is the day her boss has said she'll need to stay late for a dinner meeting with four other employees and himself. The plan is to meet at a quiet, out-of-the-way restaurant where they can discuss business.

When May arrives at the restaurant, Gerald and a woman she's never seen before are sitting in a private booth sipping wine and talking intimately. Occasionally they kiss. Gerald is so engrossed that he doesn't even see May. Because May is hoping that none of her fellow workers will recognize her husband as the man so engrossed with another woman, she does her best to keep her eyes away from the booth where Gerald and the woman are sitting. She does not interrupt them. She does not even go close to the booth where they are sitting.

That night when Gerald arrives home, May has already bathed and fed the twins and put them to bed. She confronts him as soon as he walks in the door. At first he tries to bluff her, *to deny it,* but May tells him that she has observed his liaison with her very own eyes. *Caught,* he confesses that he has had brief affairs throughout their four years of marriage, that they don't mean anything, have nothing to do with the two of them and their twins; that the marriage can continue as before. Needless to say, it can't and it didn't. Was *the yield* worth it?

Chapter III

Dexter, Dawn, and Herpes

Dawn is resistant to the idea of oral sex with Dexter, her husband of four years. He gently urges her, but still, she is opposed to the idea. As their fifth anniversary approaches, she feels her resistance wearing thin. *He's a good man, she tells herself, and we love and are faithful to one another. Maybe I'll just give it a try.*

On their fifth wedding anniversary, they celebrate with an extravagant private dinner. They share a bottle of expensive wine, a gift from friends which they have saved for this occasion. As they are preparing for bed, Dexter takes her in his arms and kisses her gently. He urges her to give it a try. "If you don't like it, you don't have to continue," he tells her. Dawn relents.

About three weeks later, Dawn feels a slight soreness in her mouth, but gives it no serious thought. A few days later as she is rinsing with mouthwash, she feels a burning sensation. She looks for the source and discovers an inflamed patch on the roof of her mouth. She makes an appointment to see her doctor. He tells her that he will culture the sore area and will call her when he knows the results.

Days later the nurse calls and leaves the following message on Dawn's answering machine: "Mrs. Everett, the doctor asked me to call and ask you to come in as soon as possible. No appointment is necessary. He'll fit you in whenever you can come."

Dawn gets the message when she arrives home from work later that day. She has been a little concerned since she noticed that sore area, now she begins to feel downright apprehensive. *Why didn't he just say what he wants?* she wonders. *Now I'll lay awake all night wondering what the message will be,* she says to herself. And she does.

The next morning Dawn calls her job to say that she has an appointment and will be at least two hours late for work. She's at the doctor's office early, even before he arrives. She is the first patient he sees that day. "Have a seat," the doctor says, indicating one of the chairs opposite his desk.

"Am I okay?" Dawn asks nervously. *I hope I'm all right,* she fleetingly thinks.

"Mrs. Everett, you've contracted herpes," he tells her. "Has your husband been tested?" he asks.

Dawn is incredulous. She knows little about herpes. She does know, however, that it can be sexually transmitted. "What do you mean?" is all she can manage just then.

It is obvious to the doctor that his diagnosis has impacted Dawn considerably. The devastation in her eyes is almost palpable in the room just then. For several minutes the doctor says nothing as Dawn stares off into space. For a few brief seconds she feels disoriented, as if she has suddenly realized that she is somewhere alone, but she's not quite sure of where or how she got there. As she begins to realize the ramifications of what she has just learned, she is distraught. She leaves the doctor's office in a daze. The news has totally disoriented her. Was *the yield* worth it?

Carla, Roderick, and Denial

Carla and Roderick have been married for eighteen years. They are both college graduates. They both have professional jobs. They have one daughter, Carrie, age twelve. They met during Roderick's senior year of college. Carla had attended college for a year, but had dropped out in order to work. She hoped to earn enough money to return to college.

When Roderick graduated, they got married and he paid Carla's tuition so that she could return to college. She became a full-time student, a very *good* one. Two-and-a-half years later, Carla graduated, with honors.

Roderick is so proud of her. When she is offered a graduate fellowship, he is the first to urge her to take it. Meanwhile, Roderick continues to advance on his job. He receives several promotions. Everyone at the job site, and especially the ladies, agree that Roderick is a great guy. He is always helpful, extremely courteous to his coworkers, a great friend and confidant.

Upon greeting any of the ladies in their circle, Roderick kisses them on the cheek; frequently he hugs them. But he doesn't greet his wife in this manner. At first Carla doesn't notice how pleasantly and affectionately he greets all of their female acquaintances as opposed to how he greets her. But eventually she does notice.

During this period, Carla is very busy with her graduate studies and does not confront her husband about what she is beginning to observe with increasing regularity. But after graduation, when she has more time to devote to the relationship, she realizes that there has been a definite cooling on his part.

She begins to wear sexier nightgowns and to experiment with costly perfumes. Frequently she asks Roderick's opinion about one fragrance or another, wanting to find a fragrance that he particularly likes on her. Roderick is always pleasant. He comments that they all smell good to him, but he never seems to notice when she wears one of the fragrances or one of the sexy nightgowns. In fact, he's stopped making sexual overtures toward her altogether.

Finally, Carla does confront him. In response he demands, "What on earth are you talking about? I work my fingers to the bone for you and Carrie! Look at all I've done for you! What do you want from me?"

Carla is incredulous. It is at this point that she realizes that Roderick is in denial. He can't admit, even to himself, that he is neglecting his wife and child while lavishing his attentions on the other women in their circle of friends.

Carla loves their daughter and wants only the best for her, and her opinion is that *the best for any child is a set of loving, united parents*. Carla loves Roderick and wants to save their marriage; to keep their family unit intact. "Maybe we should get some counseling, Roderick. Will you go to a marriage counselor with me?" Carla asks Roderick.

"You're the one with the problem, it seems. You go if you feel the need," is his only response.

Roderick, like many other Black men to whom I've spoken, refuses to go to counseling, when it is through counseling that many marriages are saved. He is afraid that counseling will reveal aspects of his personality that he desires to keep hidden, possibly even from himself. *The yield*, is it worth it?

Jewel, Steven, and the Double Life

Steven and Jewel were high school sweethearts. They were inseparable during their senior year. They were voted *Most Likely to Marry*, and they did get married during the summer following their graduation.

Neither had planned to go to college. Jewel already had a job in a local flower shop where she had worked part-time during high school. The owner liked her work and had agreed to hire her for a full-time position upon graduation from high school. Steven would soon complete training to become a long-distance trucker.

Following a long weekend honeymoon, they begin to settle into their routine. Steven is on the road for several nights each week. Jewel misses him terribly and can't wait for his return. He misses her too, and heads straight home as soon as his runs are complete.

Since they are both young, only eighteen, they agree to wait for five years before starting their family. During this period, they will save to buy a house.

Everything is proceeding as planned. To earn extra money, Steven agrees to drive longer distances. This requires him to be away from home for longer periods, sometimes as long as five to seven consecutive days.

Jewel begins to suspect that Steven is being unfaithful to her. It is also during this same period that Jewel becomes pregnant. She has morning sickness all day long. Because of it, she has to quit her job. Steven is not sympathetic. He blames her entirely for the unplanned pregnancy. He begins to stay away from home for even longer periods of time, sometimes as long as two weeks stretch. Whenever Jewel questions him about these absences, he says that he has to take longer runs now to compensate for her lost salary.

When Jewel is five months pregnant she is going through Steven's pockets, preparing to do the laundry. There is a piece of folded paper in one of the pockets. Jewel unfolds the piece of paper to reveal a phone number. She is puzzled. She decides to dial the number. Steven answers the phone. She recognizes his voice immediately. In the background she can hear soft music and what sounds like a baby crying.

"Steven? I thought you were on the road. You told me you'd be delivering a load to Tampa. You said you'd be on the road for four days this time. Steven?" *DEAD SILENCE.* "Steven?"

Eventually Steven admits that he has been living a double life for the past year, that he has fathered a child, and that Jill, the child's mother, thinks that he is a single man.

Jewel miscarries, is deeply depressed, and is now back home with her parents. *The yield*, was it worth it?

Chapter IV

Sue and No-Commitment Phil

Sue and Phil have lived together for the past ten years. From time to time they have discussed getting married. Sue has noticed, increasingly, that it is she who brings up the subject. At first she is easily diverted, not wanting to seem too aggressive. But as time passes and Phil is apparently content with the relationship as it currently exists, she becomes more and more assertive on the subject of marriage. After all, Sue is nearing forty and has spent the last ten years of her life in a relationship with a man who is still in no hurry to marry her.

That Saturday night Sue plans a romantic dinner for two. As she hears Phil's car pull up in the driveway, she puts the steaks on to broil. She lights the candles and puts the finishing touches on the table setting. Minutes later they are enjoying the dinner, the intimate conversation; the togetherness. The wine bottle is just about empty. Sue says to herself, *it's now or never*.

"Phil," she says, "let's get married this weekend. Monday is a holiday for each of us. We can get our blood tests then. My best friend, Cookie, has already offered to host the ceremony in her lovely garden, and a reception too. What'll you say?"

This has caught Phil completely off-guard. He is feeling totally relaxed. The furthest thing from his mind is getting married. Just recently he and his brother have discussed pooling their resources to buy a townhouse.

"You've already discussed this with Cookie, but not with me?" he asks, feigning incredulity. Sue tells him that she has discussed, or at least has attempted to discuss it with him, on numerous occasions.

"You interrupt, you go to the bathroom, you suddenly recall an urgent errand. You do anything to change the subject. Well, not this time! I want to know when, if not this weekend, are we going to get married? I think ten years are long enough to come to a decision. Don't you?"

But Phil refuses to make a commitment. *He isn't yet ready*, he says. Why do they *have to rush things*, he wants to know. "Aren't we doing fine just the way we are?" he asks. Sue tells him that she is no longer willing to continue their living arrangement with no wedding date to which to look forward.

Phil and Sue part company after ten years of compatible cohabitation. Is *the yield* worth it?

Amanda, Gloria, and Hubert-the-Trapped

Hubert looks and feels like a trapped animal. His mistress, Gloria, has been expecting him for more than an hour now. But his family is having an emergency; he can't get away and he can't call her either. Meanwhile, Gloria is furious. She knows that Hubert is a married man with a family, but that's never been a problem for her. Her feelings are: *if his family is no problem for him, why should I let it be one for me?*

As Gloria waits in her formal attire for Hubert to come and get dressed for the ball, he and his family sit shivering, waiting for a call from the heating and air conditioning company. It's below zero in downtown Chicago; they live in the suburbs where it is slightly colder. Their heating system stopped working over two hours ago and the temperature is *dropping by the minute*.

The telephone rings. Amanda grabs it, thinking that it's the heating company returning their call. Her "Hello" is met with *dead silence*, then the buzzing sound which indicates that the other party has disconnected.

"That's strange," Amanda says to Hubert as she hangs up the phone. "I hope that wasn't the heating company who failed to get through. That's all we need!"

"Probably just a wrong number," Hubert responds. But he is thinking, wondering *if the call was from Gloria*. She has called him before at home on a couple of occasions, but it was he who just happened to answer the phone at those times. Hubert, too, hopes that it is the heating company. But foremost on his mind right now is trying to come up with a plausible excuse that will allow him to get away. He needs to reach Gloria and at least let her know why he isn't already at her place. Amanda is wondering *why he is so jumpy.*

It is nearing ten-thirty. Hubert is feeling *desperate and trapped.* His family needs him, and he *cannot* leave them at a time like this. His mistress is dressed in her formal attire and is waiting for him to arrive. She has been waiting for more than two hours and is getting really *ticked.* Formal attire that she has rented for Hubert is still hanging in the plastic bag. She expected him hours ago, expected that the two of them would be at the ball by this time. *The yield,* is it worth it?

Joyce Willard Teal

Ruth, Josh, and Maybe Dexter

Ruth met Dexter when she began her first job teaching fifth grade in Denver. She was on the rebound from a four-year relationship with Josh. Ruth and Josh had met as college freshmen and had dated throughout college.

One week before graduation Josh had confessed to her that he has a wife and baby back home, that they are planning to attend his graduation ceremony. Ruth is heartbroken. All of the jubilance she was feeling in the approaching graduation has vanished completely.

She has so looked forward, *for four whole years,* to graduation. For almost that long, she and Josh had looked forward to it together, she had believed. They had often discussed where they'd go and what they'd do, *together,* following their graduation. She had believed, with all her heart, that their mutual plans had meant as much to him as they did to her. She simply cannot believe that he cares so little for her that he'd deliberately deceive her like he did. He'd been home with her on a number of occasions; had met her parents. Together the two of them had attended all of the important junior and senior events, and even some of the freshmen and sophomore activities. *How can I ever trust another man?* she asks herself repeatedly. *What kind of man can do what he did? What kind of human being can deny the existence of a wife and baby, lying so smoothly that one would never suspect anything contrary to what he says?* She wonders.

The two of them had frequently discussed marriage, and Ruth had no doubt that marriage was somewhere in their immediate future. Ruth loves Josh and had felt certain that her feelings were reciprocated. When she learned of his deception, she was devastated. She realizes that she has wasted four irretrievable years of her life in a relationship *with a married man*. She also realizes that she has denied herself numerous opportunities to date and get to know some of the single college men who approached her from time to time throughout the previous four years. Now she feels unable to trust what any man says to her. She has dated no one since the *breakup* with Josh. Now, in Denver, she has met Dexter, an elementary school principal. Dexter says he wants a serious relationship with Ruth. He is a nice, seemingly sincere man, but she had believed the same of Josh, unquestionably. Now Ruth can't help but wonder if he, too, has a wife and baby *back home*. *The yield*, was it worth it?

Chapter V

Ida and Disappearing Sidney

Sidney and Ida, what a pair! Ida is a junior in high school. Sidney moved to Biloxi almost two years ago. He works for a local maintenance company.

Ida's parents are rather strict, but only because they love her and want what is best for her. They prefer that she only dates boys who are in high school, as she is. "Besides," they say, "we don't know a thing about this Sidney, and remember what we've always told you, people marry only who they date."

In response Ida says, "Mom, Dad, I've got years before I can think about getting married, but Sidney's a nice guy, he works, and I like him. What more do you need to know?"

Ida frequently sneaks off with Sidney in his snazzy red convertible when her parents think she's at the library with girlfriends, or staying late for an after school activity.

When Ida misses her period, she isn't too concerned; she has always been somewhat irregular. But by the time she misses her second period, she has become a little concerned about a possible pregnancy.

She's in love with Sidney. He is her first love. She feels certain that he loves her too. She decides to confide her suspicions to him. She plans to tell him on Friday night. Her parents have consented to her request to go to a movie with him on Friday.

That Friday night they hug and kiss throughout the movie. After the movie, Sidney drives to their favorite parking spot; he reaches for her. She moves into his arms and kisses him passionately, then she says, "Wait, I've got something to tell you. I think I might be pregnant."

"Aren't you on the pill?" he questions. "I just assumed you were on the pill," he says.

"No. My parents would never allow me to take birth-control pills," Ida says. "You know how strict they are." They talk a while longer; they agree to meet for lunch at the mall the following day. They will decide what they are going to do at that time.

That Saturday morning Ida dresses carefully in her prettiest sundress. She arrives at the mall, goes to the agreed-upon food court, selects a table and sits down to wait for Sidney. It is close to noon and the court is filling rapidly. Several times Ida thinks she sees Sidney approaching, but neither time is it he. After two o'clock, she knows he isn't coming. *I wonder if he's had an accident or something on the way,* Ida says to herself.

She decides to take the bus back past his apartment. She gets off at the stop nearest his apartment. She walks the two-and-a-half blocks to his apartment complex. *His apartment is empty!* During the night Sidney has moved: *lock, stock, and barrel.*

Ida is astounded. Luckily, the pregnancy turns out to be a false alarm. But Ida's innocence and child-like trust are gone. Never again will she be able to give of herself with the assurance that her feelings are reciprocated. Was *the yield* worth it?

Wilber, Ester, and Daughter Queen

Wilber and Ester are married one beautiful spring day in late April. Several of Wilber's old girlfriends attend the wedding. He has invited them, and several of them have said, "I'll have to see it to believe it!" They know how *altar shy* Wilber is.

Wilber is fond of Ester, but from the first he has no intention of being faithful to the marriage. He is a gregarious, fun-loving guy who feels happy and content only when he has several women in his life.

Ester's thirteen-year-old daughter, Queen, likes Wilber and is pleased that he and her mother have married.

Three years have passed since their wedding day. Wilber has managed to keep the affairs and infidelities from Ester. Ester is happy in the marriage and believes that Wilber is too. And in fact, he is. The women know he's married and no longer pester him about making a commitment. He enjoys the variety he feels he needs to be content, including his wife.

Queen is now a saucy and sassy sixteen-year-old. Wilber is beginning to notice her increasingly. He winks at her when Ester isn't looking. He takes her side when she and Ester argue. Frequently he brings her little gifts when he returns from business trips.

One evening Queen arrives home late from school. Wilber is already home. He tells her that her mother has already been home, has packed an overnight bag, and has taken a flight to Cincinnati. "She'll be back tomorrow evening. Get dressed and I'll treat you to dinner out," he tells her.

Queen is overjoyed. She sprints up the stairs and puts on her most *grownup* dress. She borrows a pair of her mother's shoes: *heels*. She sneaks a spray of her mother's expensive perfume.

Wilber takes her to an exclusive restaurant. He lets her order a glass of wine with the admonition, "This'll be our first secret." As they leave the restaurant, he drapes his arm, casually, around her shoulders. When they arrive home, Queen goes directly upstairs to her room. She undresses and gets into the shower. She is feeling woozy from the unaccustomed wine.

As she steps out of the shower and reaches for the towel, it isn't where she left it. Wilber has it. "Come and get it," he chants. "Come and get it; come and get it."

Queen is feeling thoroughly sober now. *Something is terribly wrong.* She knows Wilber shouldn't be seeing her like this. She knows this isn't right. She runs back into the bathroom, locks the door, and snatches one of the guest towels from the rack.

Meanwhile she hears Wilber moving around in the hallway. "Wilber!" she yells through the door, "what are you doing out there?"

"I'm trying to give you the towel so you can dry off. Come on, take it."

"I don't need it. I've already dried off. Go away, Wilber!" Queen shouts.

"What's going on here?" Ester asks as she comes up the stairs. She is observing the towel in Wilber's hand. Queen opens up the bathroom door wrapped in one of the guest towels. She tells her mother exactly what has transpired.

"You bastard!" Ester screams. "I should have you arrested for giving alcohol to a minor! Pack you bags and get out! Now! Tonight!"

Ester had recently begun to suspect Wilber's infidelities. She had faked the trip to Cincinnati just to see what Wilber would do if he believed she would be out of the city overnight. But she had not suspected this. She'd never suspected he'd stoop this low. *The yield*, was it worth it?

Sheena, Boyd, and Liz

Sheena's second marriage is to Boyd, a preacher. If anybody will be moral, ethical, and truthful, a preacher will, she thought.

They are married in his church by one of his minister friends. His congregation gives them a big send-off. The honeymoon in Palm Springs is fabulous.

They return home and begin to settle into their routine. Boyd's ministerial responsibilities keep him busy; he is rarely home. But Sheena had expected this. They had dated for more than three years before the marriage, so she pretty much knew what to expect. Prior to the marriage, however, no matter how busy Boyd was, he always made time for Sheena. But after the marriage, with increasing frequency, he leaves her home alone. He rarely asks her to go with him, and when she asks to accompany him, he always gives some reason why she has to stay behind.

Sometimes he takes on responsibilities that could have and should have been delegated to others on the ministerial staff, just to give himself what he considers legitimate reasons for staying away from home. He always rationalizes: *he is helping to ease the burdens of his fellow workers. He is a man of God; he has a duty to do all that he can for his parishioners.* Never once did he think: *I owe my new wife allegiance too. She deserves some of my time and attention.*

The new member, Liz, is beautiful, and she seems dedicated to the Lord's work. She sings in two of the choirs; she serves on several boards and is at the church three or four nights every week and sometimes more. She and Boyd worked closely on several projects.

One night they are the last two people to leave the church. As they walk out to their cars, Boyd realizes he's left his briefcase in his office. When he expresses this to Liz she says, "I'll walk back in with you." As they re-enter the office, they kiss. No one could have said who turned first to whom. They separate, then they kissed again. Both seem dazed, disoriented, as if neither had expected this to happen.

After this incident, they try to avoid one another, but it was inevitable that they will be required to do some work at the church together. They are on many of the same boards and serve on some of the same committees.

The next time they end up alone together, neither fights it. They begin to meet in places where nobody knows either of them. They become lovers. Now his wife sees even less of him, and when they are together, he is already saturated from his liaisons with Liz. He no longer is interested in being intimate with his wife.

Sheena begins to suspect Boyd of being unfaithful to her. She knows him to be a very virile man, and since he isn't making love to her she reasons, then he is making love to someone else.

It doesn't take her long to confirm that this is indeed so. Sheena is shattered. *If you can't trust a preacher, a professed man of God, who can you trust?* she asks herself repeatedly. Was *the yield* worth it?

Chapter VI

Erica, Sam. and His Need for Freedom

Erica feels dazed, disoriented, as if a rug has been quickly snatched from under her feet when she wasn't even aware that a rug was there. Samuel, her husband of twenty-seven years, has just told her that he needs some freedom. She has trouble processing what she has just heard. She didn't even know that he had no freedom. But I'm getting ahead of myself. Allow me to digress, to begin at the beginning of her heartache.

Sam and Eri have raised two daughters. Both girls have recently graduated from historically Black colleges. Their youngest, Dawn, is getting married in four days. Sam and Eri are packing, preparing for the trip out-of-state, to the wedding.

The phone rings, but when Eri says, "Hello," no one answers. She knows someone is still there because she can hear the quiet breathing. No one says anything, then the caller hangs up. Eri too hangs up, and resumes her packing.

"Who was that?" Sam asks.

"Beats me," Eri responds.

It's getting late and they have not yet eaten dinner. Sam suggests they take a break and go out for burgers. Eri agrees. When they return, Sam goes upstairs to resume his packing. Eri goes into the kitchen and picks up the phone to check their messages. She is expecting Dawn to call and to inquire about their expected time of departure. But this is the message that she hears: "Sam Burke, get your ass over here right now!"

Eri is astounded. *Who feels familiar enough with her husband to leave such a message? Who feels confident enough to call her home and leave a message such as this for her husband?* she wonders.

"Sam," Eri says, still feeling baffled, "there's a message for you from some woman."

"What does it say?" he inquires. She hands him the phone and tells him to listen for himself.

Sam listens for a brief time, then he deletes the message. He can see that lying at this point will be an insult to Eri's intelligence. He confesses to being involved with the woman, Keri, for almost a year now. During the confrontation, he also admits to having had numerous affairs throughout the twenty-seven years of marriage.

"It's not that I don't love you," he tells Eri. "I do, and I always will. It's just that this sort of got out of hand. She knows that I'm married. I've never lied to anyone about that, but I need some freedom."

Prior to the immediate past confrontation, Erica thought they had an ideal marriage. She loves Samuel; she loves their life together. She has always truly believed that Sam feels the same way. Never once has she felt that he isn't happy and content, fulfilled within the marriage, as she herself has been.

Now she begins to doubt everything they have shared. She begins to examine past events, past incidents, in light of this new awareness. She begins to wonder what he is thinking during silences that were once so comfortable between them (at least she has felt comfortable during them).

The novel experience of packing for a beloved daughter's wedding, which had held such pleasure, is now ruined for her, a chore. She does not even want to go, especially not in the same car with Sam. *But I won't ruin Dawn's big day. I'm not that selfish. Dawn worships Sam. I could never shatter her happiness just because mine has been shattered. This should be one of the happiest days of Dawn's life*, Eri says to herself. *All of the girls' lives they've looked forward to walking down the aisle on Sam's arm on their wedding day. I couldn't live with myself if I were responsible for ruining that for either of them. I'll put my feelings aside, on hold. I'll bury my resentment for Dawn's sake*, she tells herself. And she does.

Dawn has a beautiful wedding. She and Eric depart for their honeymoon amidst showers of confetti and well wishes. Eri wants this for her. She has never had any trouble making needed sacrifices for the sake of her family. Sam and the girls have been her whole life, her primary reason for living. This is the main reason why Sam's betrayal is so painful. She'd never doubted his loyalty, his protectiveness of her and the girls.

Now she goes to bed each night and rises each morning with a heavy heart. She thinks constantly of all the shared experiences they've had as a family. *Was he wishing at those times that he could be elsewhere? Was some-*

one else waiting for him and wondering when he'd be able to break away from his family? she wonders. Her heart is a brick in her chest cavity. She must eat whatever she swallows past the lump in her throat. Her feet have lost their spring. Her mind wanders when she tries to read a book. She has no idea what the page she just finished said. *So this is how it feels to be heartbroken*, she realizes. *I never knew this kind of pain existed*, she recognizes.

"I'll have to tell them," Eri confides to Elana, her best friend since grade school. "I've put it off as long as I can because I know how both the girls feel about Sam. It's going to hurt them deeply, but not as deeply as hearing it from someone else. And I know Sam will never tell them. He doesn't have the guts to do it, yet he says that he doesn't want to change, doesn't even know if he can change, even if he tries. So you see, the girls have to be told," she concludes.

Three months have passed since Dawn's wedding day. Diedra drove down to Dawn's house and the two of them drove together to their parents' home. Eri and the girls are now relaxing on the king-sized bed in the master suite. "Where's Dad?" Diedra inquires.

Without responding to Dawn's inquiry Eri says, "I have something to tell you girls." And tell them she does. She ends with, "So I don't know how much longer Sam and I will be together. There are legal matters that must be handled. He says he needs his freedom."

Eri can see the sadness, the denial, in the girls' eyes. Both girls cry; neither had any idea. To them, Sam is like a god. He is the first man they ever knew; the first man they had loved. In their hearts, he could do no wrong. They alternate between disbelief and rage; yet they know that this is not something their mother would tell them if it were not entirely true. Eri is heartbroken, crushed. The girls' faith in loyalty to family, which both their parents instilled, is now shaken. Their image of fatherhood, and of their father, is forever altered. *The yield*, was it worth it?

Eunice and Eugene, the Weekend Alcoholic

Eugene is a weekend alcoholic. He hardly drinks at all during the week, but when he leaves work on Friday he starts, and he doesn't stop until well past midnight on Sunday.

Eunice has tried, repeatedly, to get him to go to A.A., but he declares adamantly, *that there's no need, she's making a mountain out of a molehill. He can stop any time he wants. He does it to unwind. A man needs to relax after an exhausting week. Doesn't he?*

Eunice and Eugene have four children: Bary, Beth, Erin and Edna. They range in age from fifteen to nine. They're all aware of their dad's drinking because he's never hidden it from them. His own dad drank heavily during his pre-teen and adolescent years, and he was well aware of it. So this, to Eugene, is normal behavior. "Eunice is the problem," he laments to one of his drinking buddies. "There's nothing wrong with a man unwinding after slaving all week for *the man*," he concludes.

And there isn't. But there is definitely something wrong with the method he's chosen to unwind. The children are afraid of him when he's drinking; they try to stay out of his path. They are ashamed to invite their friends over during weekends for fear of embarrassment. His wife worries every time he cranks up the car during weekends. She is on pins and needles until he pulls back up into the driveway, hoping and praying he'll not be hit and will not hit someone while he is *driving under the influence*. She's tried hiding his keys, but he's so unreasonable when he's intoxicated that she wants to spare the children, and herself, the aggravation of having to deal with that situation ever again: *the threats, the profanity,* things he'd never do or say when he hasn't been drinking. Eunice works part time during the week, but it is hard for her to relax, even when she's off, dreading the coming weekend.

Now Erin, their thirteen-year-old son, has started sneaking beer. At first, it is just a can every once in a while, to emulate his dad, then two, then three; later, as many as he thinks he might be able to get away with. Still later he progresses to sneaking small amounts of the stronger liquors. Now he does so every day, to the extent that Eugene would be able to detect it if he were not so accustomed to having his hoard left undisturbed, except by himself, for so many years. But because this is so, he just doesn't pay any attention from one weekend to the next. He merely assumes that everything is as he left it, as it has always been.

Erin arranges the cans and bottles so his dad won't notice that a few are missing. Sometimes he adds a little water to a bottle to replace what he's taken. And so the cycle is perpetuated. *The yield,* is it worth it?

Luther and Lacy, Perfection?

Luther and Lacy grew up together. They played together as children. They were teased about being girlfriend and boyfriend long before either of them thought about such things. Being in the same grade, at the same school, they frequently had classes together. Luther was Lacy's first boyfriend and she was his first girlfriend. They share many happy memories. When it was time for their senior prom, there was no question that they would attend it together. And they did.

Things should have been perfect for them. But they weren't. Lacy was unaware that Luther was growing up in a household where he frequently saw and heard his father disrespect his mother. His dad spoke rudely and condescendingly to his mother, he was inconsiderate of her feelings, and he often didn't come home for two to three consecutive days, with no explanation when he did return. Luther observed and internalized this behavior throughout his boyhood, and accepted it as normal, *as just the way things were.*

Lacy will begin nursing school in the fall. She plans to live at home instead of the dormitory. That way, she'll have only tuition to pay. She and Luther have promised one another they'll save as much as they can so that as soon as he completes his stint in the Airforce, they can begin their life together as a married couple.

Luther completes basic training and is granted a thirty-day leave of absence. It is during this period that Lacy encounters Luther's rudeness for the first time. She doesn't know what to make of it, but when he apologizes profusely, she accepts his apology. She loves him. She told herself that *he is in an uptight frame of mind about the overseas tour of duty,* and he was genuinely repentant.

Luther's overseas tour lasts for a two-year period. During this period, Lacy becomes a Licensed Vocational Nurse. The two of them plan to marry upon his return to the States. They write faithfully to one another, discussing their plans and declaring their undying love for one another.

The wedding is small, but beautiful. Both families and a few close friends attend. The bride and groom spend their honeymoon in Hawaii. Luther spent a brief period of R & R there while in the Airforce and he had written and told Lacy how beautiful and scenic it is.

They have agreed it would be the perfect place for their honeymoon. Their week there was marred by only one incident. On their fourth day in Hawaii, Lacy awakes late one morning to find Luther's side of the bed empty. She looks around for a note, *but there is no note.* He doesn't return until nearly six o'clock that evening.

"Where have you been? I've been worried sick about you," Lacy exclaimed as soon as Luther walked in the door. She felt distraught, thinking that all sorts of things must've happened for him to be gone all day like that with no call or note or anything.

"Nowhere; just out looking around," Luther responds with a frown. He is annoyed that Lacy is questioning him. He feels that a man shouldn't have to answer to anyone for his comings and goings. Lacy is so happy that none of the things she'd imagined had happened, that she lets the subject drop.

Following their honeymoon, they return to say their good-byes to their families and friends. They will be living in Arlington, a suburb a few miles away from their hometown. Lacy already has a job at a hospital there. Luther plans to begin job-hunting the following Monday morning. He has already made a few inquiries and completed a few applications. He has been trained to repair computers while in the Air Force. Before long, he has a job repairing them for a major computer firm.

Luther and Lacy settle into their jobs and into their married life. They both have good jobs which they enjoy. They have unlimited access to one another, something each has longed for since their teen years. Things should have been perfect for them. But they aren't. Luther begins coming home late from work. Initially, it is only an hour or two, then it becomes three, four. It progresses to after midnight several nights each week. He offers no explanation and makes it blatantly obvious that he resents being questioned about it. He feels that Lacy has no right to question him. *He works steadily; he brings his money home. What more can she want? Doesn't he have a right to use his spare time as he sees fit?* He responds rudely to Lacy's questions. He feels that it is a man's right to come home, or to not come home, as it pleases him, and at whatever time he chooses.

Coming home late with no explanation was just the tip of the iceberg. Before long, Luther begins staying out all night. At first it is only once in a while; later it becomes two, even three consecutive nights. He never offers an explanation for these absences; he makes it abundantly clear that he resents being asked about these times.

Lacy becomes a nervous wreck. She sleeps poorly. Her job performance suffers. Her supervisor, a kind and understanding elderly registered nurse, takes her aside and asks her what has happened to the wonderful, enthusiastic young nurse she recently hired. Lacy tearfully shares with her *her* situation with Luther. Nurse Colby advises Lacy to take a day day off, get some sleep, and to seek some professional counseling. "It's obvious to me that you can't continue at this pace. To be alert you need sleep and rest. You can't, in fact, nobody can rest under the circumstances you've just described to me. You're a good nurse, with excellent potential. Don't squander it by coming to work already tired and worn out from lack of rest. I'm not the only one who's noticed the changes in you. But I'm probably the only one who has noticed who is willing to alert you like I'm doing. Do you understand what I mean?" she asks.

"I do," Lacy says, "and I really appreciate your understanding. I intend to make some changes. I really do love nursing, and I have been hoping I could get into that registered nursing program the hospital is offering. But I know I'll have to do something about my personal life before I can even think about that," Lacy shares with Nurse Colby.

Luther doesn't come home the following night, but Lacy takes a sleeping pill so that she will not have to go to work totally exhausted, as she has done so often of late. The next evening when he does come home, Lacy tells him that she needs to speak with him about their problem. "What problem?" he asks. "We wouldn't have a problem if you'd just accept me the way I am," he states belligerently. Lacy tries to explain to him that it isn't normal for a man, or woman, to expect to disappear for days at a time without informing his or her mate that he or she will be gone and when he or she can be expected to return. Luther looks at her as if she is speaking a foreign language, but he makes no response.

Now whenever Luther does come home, the two of them quarrel constantly.

Whenever he tries to be nice to her, or to make love to her, all she can think about are those times when he doesn't come home, doesn't call to say he won't be home, and his rudeness when she asks about those times. By their fifth wedding anniversary, they are hardly speaking to one another. Now Luther blames her for why he doesn't like being home. "When I'm here, all you do is bitch!" he yells during their latest argument. "Why do you want me here?"

"You know what?" she responds hotly, "I don't!" And she suddenly realizes that she doesn't, that it doesn't make any sense for her to want him to come home so they can argue, *which is all they do now when the two of them are together.*

The next time Luther doesn't come home, Lacy packs her things and moves back to her parents' home. Luther calls and declares his undying love for her, that he wants her back. He tells all of their friends that he will always love her, that he has no interest in any other woman. *The yield,* was it worth it?

Chapter VII

Matthew, Mable, and Discontent

Matthew and Mable have been married for thirty-seven years. Their adult children, Matt, Jr. and Mamie, are thirty and twenty-seven years old respectively.

During the early years of their marriage, they struggled along happily together, she an elementary school teacher, he a high school football coach. They shared everything: successes and failures, highs and lows; laughter and tears, families and friends.

Both of them wanted children, so when Mable gave birth to Matt, Jr., they were thrilled. Money was tight, but they both agreed that Mable should take a year off to give their son the best possible start.

Being a good money manager, Mable knew how to economize, so they did quite well on just Matt's salary. Sometimes Matt earned extra money officiating, refereeing games at schools in nearby towns. In fact, Matt was gaining quite a good reputation as a fair and skilled officiator. He was even offered the chance to train in order to become one of the professional referees, but he turned it down because he didn't want to spend that much time away from Mable and Matt, Jr. Mamie had not yet been born when this happened.

Little Matt grew healthy and robust. The family was happy and content. Mable returned to work when Jr. was a year old. Since they had grown accustomed to living on one salary, they were able to save quite handsomely.

During the following two years, they bought a house and began furnishing it. They replaced their older car, a twenty year old station wagon from Mable's college days, with an almost new Volvo. They began to plan for their second child.

When Mamie was born, almost exactly three years after Matt, Jr., they felt that their family was complete. Their relationship had matured, right along with them. It was rich and satisfying, and secure. They felt truly blessed. They led very busy lives. With chauffeuring their growing children to and from their activities and keeping up with the demands of a growing family as well as fulfilling job obligations, they hardly had time for each other. But no matter how busy they were, they always made time for each other; they found time to be together. Before either could believe it, Matt, Jr. was beginning his senior year of high school and applying to colleges.

The years passed pleasantly, and much too quickly. Matt, Jr. graduated from college and began working in his chosen profession. Mamie got married during her senior year of college. She and Harold eloped, but each graduated, right on schedule.

Now Matt and Mable have come full circle. They are right back where they started: just the two of them, and Mable is delighted. They have worked hard together to give their children the best that life has to offer: *a loving home; deeply embedded personal morals; a stable, nurturing home environment with two loving, committed parents.* Now it is time for the two of them to relax and enjoy life together as a couple. She envisions the two of them together on a cruise taking a long vacation; sleeping as long in the mornings as they want. She loves Matt more than ever and is elated to be free to devote herself fully to their relationship.

Matt, however, does not share Mable's ideas of what retirement means. When she moves into his arms during early mornings, he now makes excuses, mentioning some pending obligation; feigns sleep or fatigue. Initially, Mable does not think anything of it. The two of them have always been straight with one another. If Matt tells her that he has an obligation, then he has one. It has never even occurred to her to doubt his honesty. *Not ever.* She's never had any reason to do so. But as time passes, she begins to miss their shared passion and the closeness that it has fostered. She now begins to notice that he never reaches out to her, never even hugs or kisses her anymore. She has no idea to what to attribute this behavior. After all, she reasons, *we have been married for almost forty years; maybe this is just a natural progression, the way things are supposed to be.* But still, *she misses the intimacy they shared for so many years. She misses the way they'd look into one another's eyes across a crowded room and know exactly what the other was thinking. She misses the way he'd squeeze her hand when he wanted her to make some excuse, legitimate or otherwise, so they could leave a party or other gathering. She misses the way they'd talk about anything on their minds,* without reserve. She misses the way they'd snuggle early mornings when they'd have a day off. She misses the way Matt would sneak up behind her when she was at the kitchen sink making dinner, and kiss her behind the ear. She keeps thinking of all these things, and more. She tries to seduce him; it doesn't work. She tries to talk to him; it doesn't work. She tries to get him to go to counseling with her; that doesn't work either. He tells her that he doesn't have a problem. "If you have a problem, then you go talk to someone," he says.

Now, for the first time in thirty-seven years of married life, Mable is unhappy, discontented. Matt, who has never treated her unkindly, has begun speaking harshly to her. Unpredictably, he lashes out, verbally, when something quite minor in her opinion, displeases him. Mable wonders what has gone wrong; what has happened to the man whom she has adored for well over half of her lifetime. She wishes he would just talk to her, share his feelings with her. But he won't; *she is so unhappy.*

"If he is unable to perform sexually, I can live with that," Mable confides to a close friend. "But what I can't handle is this loss of closeness, this loss of sharing that I thought nearly a half century of marriage assured. I don't believe he's having an affair, but even that might be preferable to this. How can a man change so, metamorphose, right before my eyes, and yet I miss the transformation? But its results are amazingly clear. I don't know what to do; where to turn. I wouldn't even know how to begin to think of my life, minus Matt, yet I feel like the Matt I've known and loved is no longer here. It's like living with a stranger now. I never know what'll set him off. He never used to be like that. He was always the one to tease me out of my moods. I feel confused, dismayed. *The yield*, is it worth it?

Tisha, Tomas, and Yvonne

Tisha got pregnant during her senior year of college. Since she and Tomas had been dating for a year, and were in love, they decided that marriage was the perfect solution.

Tomas had come from a small town in Mississippi. He lived on campus at the small Texas college where he and Tisha met and fell in love. The college was in Tisha's hometown; she lived at home with her parents and younger brothers and sisters. Tomas was frequently invited to share meals with the family. They all liked and thought highly of him.

Tisha has two older brothers, one of whom is married to Yvonne. Yvonne and Brad have three small children. Tisha and Tomas frequently babysit their children. Sometimes the four of them go out together on weekends, or they and all three children pile into Brad's old van and take in a drive-in movie. They enjoy each other's company and spend a good deal of their leisure time together.

Tomas graduated from college only a few months before Terrence, their son, was born. Tisha graduated only a few months later, that summer. The two of them are happy, but Tisha can't put Carmen out of her mind. She knows that Carmen was Tomas's high school sweetheart. Carmen is also the daughter of Tomas's parents' closest friends. Both sets of parents totally approved of the relationship between Tomas and Carmen, and had encouraged it for years. They fully expected that Tomas and Carmen would marry at some unspecified date in the future.

It isn't that they don't like Tisha. In fact, they do like her. Tisha is a beautiful and sweet young woman. No one can really know her and not like her. But they had counted on Tomas and Carmen getting married, that it would happen. Both sets of parents just took for granted that it would happen. Carmen and Tomas had played together as children. Their parents are close, and had wanted as well as expected that a closeness would develop between their children. *And it did.*

During their freshman year when Tisha had known Tomas only peripherally, Carmen had frequently been invited to Texas to accompany Tomas to formal dances, banquets, and other campus social events. This is how Tisha knows about her. It was common knowledge on the campus that Carmen and Tomas were sort of unofficially engaged; that their parents expected them to marry at some future time.

When Tomas approached Tisha for their first date, she thought about Carmen, but decided that mentioning her at that point would be tantamount to asking him to declare his intentions toward her, and she didn't feel good about that, so she said nothing.

"It's only a movie and maybe a hotdog later," she told a good friend, Mae, who had reminded her of Carmen's existence. "What's the big deal if he does already have a girlfriend? He hasn't asked me, and if he does, I'm not sure that I want to be his girl."

Well, he didn't ask her that night, but they enjoyed each other's company immensely. Before long, they are thought of as *an item* on the campus. From time to time Carmen is mentioned in their conversations, but Tomas makes it clear that he is free to do whatever he wants with whomever he wants, that there is no commitment between Carmen and him. So Tisha thought it wise to let the subject drop.

Meanwhile, their relationship is becoming serious. They are dating one another exclusively; they are spending all of their leisure time, and much of their study time together. They are in love.

Now that they're married and their son is almost two years old, Tisha has relaxed. She no longer feels threatened by Carmen, and she shouldn't. It isn't Carmen who is the threat. But neither should she relax, because Yvonne and Brad have begun sneaking around, meeting in hotels and motels.

Because they all spend a good deal of time together, Tisha suspects nothing. In fact, her first indication that something is untoward has to do with their finances. Suddenly, their money is no longer lasting from payday to payday. That should not have been.

They both work professionally and earn good salaries. Their bills are budgeted for; their savings are automatically deducted. A specific amount has been allocated as *running money* for each of them; miscellaneous expenses are provided for. This system has worked well during the two and a half years of their marriage. Now, for reasons unknown to Tisha, it is no longer working.

Tisha and Tomas began to quarrel about money, something they'd never done. Tomas secretly began making withdrawals from their savings account. Occasionally, he'd make a withdrawal from Terrence's educational fund. He used this extra money for his liaisons with Yvonne. Sometimes he'd ask Tisha for money, something that had been unnecessary heretofore.

One day Tisha leaves work early because she has a headache. On the way home, she has to go past Yvonne and Brad's apartment. Tomas's pickup is parked right in front of the apartment. *Why is he there*? Tisha wonders, as she continues on her way home, head pounding, mind on a remedy for the pain.

When she arrives home, she takes aspirins from the medicine cabinet, still thinking about seeing Tomas's pickup at the Glacer's apartment. She decides to call him at work, assuming he has returned, and to ask him about it. She feels no suspicion at this juncture, merely curiosity.

Tisha places the call and is told that Tomas has already left for the day. She toys with the idea of asking his secretary what time he left work, but decides against it, not wanting to arouse her suspicions unduly.

When Tomas arrives home, Tisha asks him why he left work early and why he was at Brad and Yvonne's apartment earlier that evening. At this point Tisha realizes there could be hundreds of reasons why, but when Tomas looks startled that she knows he was there, she realizes that something is amiss. Faced with Tisha's awareness, Tomas confesses to having a six-month affair with Yvonne, that the extra money he'd needed had been used to finance it.

Now Tomas and Tisha are getting a divorce. Tisha's parents, sisters, and brothers have all lost respect for Tomas. Terrence cries constantly, asking about his dad. He now wets the bed, something he almost never did before. Yvonne and Brad are estranged. *The yield*, was it worth it?

Nikki, Shree, and Mike

Nikki and Shree are both pregnant. They are both pregnant by the same guy, Michael. Nikki is two months pregnant. Shree is five weeks pregnant. But I'm getting ahead of the story. Let me regress and tell the whole story.

Mike met Shree at his company's annual picnic. He and Nikki had planned to attend it together, but Nikki isn't feeling well. She is pregnant, but she isn't aware of it at this time. She has waited until the last minute to call Mike, hoping he'll say that he doesn't want to go without her, that he'll come over to her apartment and heat some soup for her, anything that might validate for her how he feels about their relationship. Instead, what he says is, "I'm sorry to hear that; I'll call you later." Needless to say, she was quite disappointed.

Nikki and Mike have been dating for the past six months, and she is in love with Mike. He has told her he loves her too. She is dating him exclusive- and she believes that he is dating her exclusively. He isn't. Neither has actually said so to the other, but they have discussed sexually transmitted diseases and the importance behaving responsibly.

She'd just assumed that was tantamount to a declaration of one, exclusive relationship at a time. That is certainly what she'd meant, and how she behaved.

Well, Mike went on to the picnic. He was there for less than an hour when a tall, beautiful, young woman got out of an old station wagon, along with her parents. He recognized the middle-aged couple, both of whom had recently retired from the company. He vaguely remembered hearing that they had a daughter who was away at college, but he'd never seen her previously.

They waved to him and he walked over to where they were. They introduced the two of them. He fell in step with the threesome and helped them to find a shady spot to spread the old quilt they had brought along with them.

"Let's get cold drinks for everyone," Mike says to Shree after her parents are relaxing comfortably on the quilt. She agrees, and they head in the direction of the food and drinks. By the time they return with the drinks, Shree has ascertained that Mike is alone; she and her parents invite Mike to share their quilt with them.

Before the picnic ends, Mike has invited Shree to a concert that is scheduled to take place during the following week. *He's polite, and he's certainly good-looking*, Shree says to herself as they head for their respective cars. She has agreed to the concert date.

Meanwhile, Nikki feels sure that Mike will call or just stop by to check on her after the picnic. She has showered and put on the new shorts set she's bought to wear to the picnic. She has also put on a little make-up. She wants to look her best if he just happens to drop by unannounced. But Mike doesn't call, so she decides to call him. "I'm bushed," he tells her. "I think I'll stay in tonight."

This is a Saturday night. Nikki and Mike have spent the past ten immediate Saturday nights together. At first they'd go to movies, to concerts, to museums; for long drives in the country. But as they got to know each other better, they spent Saturday nights at one or the other's apartment. Sometimes they'd prepare dinner together; at other times they'd order take-out. Eventually they'd end up in bed together. Nikki genuinely cares for Mike, and he has led her to believe that he cares for her too.

The following Saturday night, Nikki just assumes she'll hear from Mike. She has spoken with him briefly during the week. But still, he does not call. He has a concert date with Shree, but of course Nikki has no knowledge of his plans. What Nikki does know though, is that she is pregnant. When feelings of nausea persists her doctor suggests a pregnancy test. The test confirmed his and Nikki's suspicions. Now Nikki is torn between calling Mike and telling him about the pregnancy and waiting to see if he will call her. She is not yet ready to believe that he will just stop calling her with no explanation given.

It has now been several weeks since the company picnic. Mike and Shree have gone out every weekend since the picnic and have even gone out to dinner several times during the week. Recently they have become intimate.

Shree is twenty years old. Mike is her first, serious, adult relationship. She's in love with him. He likes her too, *but Mike loves only himself.* Of late he has begun to feel that Shree is becoming too possessive, too expectant. He does not want any woman to feel that his weekends are exclusively her domain, *that he is committed.* He has no intentions, nor desire, to make a commitment to any woman. Mike says jokingly to his buddies, "There are too many beautiful women out there looking for a handsome, hard-working Black man like me, and I intend to be easily found!"

Mike, like so many other Black men, is toying with other people's lives, playing games with other people's emotions. It is certainly okay to be unready to make a commitment. In fact, a person should not make a commitment if he or she is not ready to make the necessary sacrifices to honor it. But it is not okay to lead others on, to lead others to believe that you love them solely for your own selfish motives, with your hidden agenda already intact. That is inexcusable, but it is precisely what Mike has done. Now two new lives have been created, two trusting, sincere women violated. *The yield,* is it worth it?

Chapter VIII

Stewart Stealing

Stewart has just been arrested, handcuffed right in front of of his family. Greta, his wife of eleven years, and their children, Chad, Chanda, and Chip, are terrified, distraught. The children are hysterical, inconsolable, and Greta is in no condition to console them. She's as bewildered as the children, and even more frightened, if that's possible. They are sure there's been some mistake, but still, seeing their beloved husband and father handcuffed and forced into a police car is more than they can stand.

Stewart has worked for a leading carpet manufacturer for the past twelve years. He was working there when he met Greta. He started working for the company right out of high school. Stewart's shift is the four to midnight shift. He prefers this particular shift because it allows him to have his days free. He's able to go on occasional field trips with the children and to go to the school when one of them is in a program. It allows him to take them for dental and doctor appointments. Greta, who is a registered nurse, says the shift has been a godsend for her and the children. They're all devoted to Stewart, and he loves them too.

For years, Stewart worked honestly at his job, got to work on time, left when his shift was over; occasionally worked overtime. One night recently he was approached by two guys who worked the day shift. He knew them by sight, only casually. The guys told him that they could be instrumental in helping him to *make some real money*. They and several of the other workers have been stealing from the company for years. When rolls of carpet were loaded onto company trucks, no one would be the wiser, they thought, if one of their trucks got a few of those rolls loaded onto it. And for years they got away with it.

For the past six months, the company has been under new management. The new manager has asked for, and gotten, an audit. The audit has revealed irregularities that have lead to their suspicions. As a result, additional security persons have been hired, expressly for the four to midnight shift. This has all been done very *hush, hush*. Only key personnel are involved and only they are privy to the details.

When Joe and Carl approach Stewart, they know nothing about these new developments. They are aware that the company's management changed, about six months prior. And they have *laid low* for several weeks. Now they feel sure that it is safe to resume their private operations.

Stewart thinks about all the things he can do with the extra money. He agrees to meet with Joe and Carl the following day during his lunch hour to hear the details. He meets with them and listens to their spiel. His response is, "Count me in."

For the past several weeks a hidden security camera has recorded everything that takes place on the loading docks between 7p.m. and midnight. Results reveal who is doing the stealing as well as how it is being accomplished. Now warrants have been issued for the arrest of each man involved.

Stewart's family is devastated. They can't believe he'd do anything that would deprive them of his presence in their lives. They can't believe he'd involve himself in any venture that could deprive himself of their presence in his life. *The yield,* was it worth it?

Lauren, Luis, and Dr. Pat

"You know, I worked six years to help Luis through medical school, and now that he's made it, he's trading me in for a newer model. I just can't believe it, yet I know it's true," Lauren confides to a close friend. It hurts so much to know that he can do this. Realizing that he is not the caliber of man that I always believed him to be hurts as much as the betrayal," she concludes.

Luis and Lauren met during their junior year of college. They couldn't wait to get married, and they didn't. They sneaked off one weekend and returned as husband and wife. They had discussed it beforehand and had agreed they'd both complete the term, then Lauren would leave school, get a job, and help Luis get through college, then medical school.

Little Lisa wasn't planned, but neither was really upset when they learned that she was on the way. And when she was born, both were delighted with her. She was a healthy and beautiful baby. Luis and Lauren couldn't seem to stop smiling, and before long, little Lisa was smiling right along with them.

Lauren returned to work when Lisa was only four weeks old. As the family's only breadwinner, it was necessary, and she didn't mind. They were in love. They had limitless access to each other. They had a beautiful and healthy daughter; they were looking forward to a great future.

On the day that Luis graduated from *med* school, Lisa had her fifth birthday. They were elated with their accomplishments. They had worked hard together, and all three of them felt good about the parts they'd played. Even little Lisa had made a special effort not to disturb Daddy when he was studying.

Frequently, he'd pick her up from the sitter. They'd each talk about their day. He'd give her snack, then he'd hit the books. Long before Lisa could read, she did a lot of *studying*, like Daddy, surrounded by her books.

And she did learn to read by the time she was four, probably because of all that *studying*, Luis frequently said laughingly to Lauren. Together they'd sometimes make dinner for *Mommy*. They were truly bonded, and they truly loved one another.

The family grew and prospered. Luis completed all preliminary practicums and was now a full-fledged doctor, on staff at two local hospitals. He had also acquired part ownership in a private clinic with two other doctors, both of whom were young and ambitious. They'd borrowed heavily to finance their venture; it was a thriving business in a wealthy suburb, so it was paying off, *big time*. Lauren continued to work for another year, but when she became pregnant with the baby they'd both been hoping for, she gave notice that she'd be leaving her job.

Laurence, their son, was born one frosty, December morning. Luis delivered the baby himself, and how delighted they all were, even little Lisa who had specifically ordered a baby brother.

When Laurence was six months old, the family moved into their dream home, the one Luis and Lauren had designed themselves and had *had* built to their specifications. The clinic was busier than ever, and each of the partners agreed they needed additional help. They decided to seek a fourth partner, someone who could afford to *buy in*, pay his or her fair share, and handle a fair share of the burgeoning workload.

The partners did not lack for potential associates, hopefuls, but they knew they couldn't afford to make a mistake. After many months of painstaking interviewing and reference checking, they settled on Dr. Patricia Royce-Burne, a pediatrician. She was from a family of doctors, with a father, an aunt, and two uncles who were also physicians. As an only child, she owed no medical school loans; she had a nice nest egg, left to her by a deceased aunt, which she used to buy into the practice. In addition, she brought to the clinic staff expertise in childhood ailments and diseases, something it had lacked heretofore.

The partners had chosen well, it seemed. Everyone loved Dr. Pat, as she was affectionately called by the children, as well as the other doctors on the staff. Dr. Pat usually arrived at the clinic each morning before any of the other doctors got there. As a divorcee, she was the only one of them who didn't have family obligations. Luis's two other partners, Earl and Stanley, both had wives who also worked professionally, so they sometimes had to drop their kids off et sitters, or at school. Since Lauren didn't work Luis never had to perform these duties. This allowed him to arrive at the clinic earlier than either Earl or Stanley. He and Dr. Pat just sort of drifted into the habit of having coffee together each morning. They'd discuss professional interests, and sometimes local political happenings. They began looking forward to these early morning chats. One or the other began to bring a danish to share with the coffee. Now they had coffee together each morning. During these times, there seemed between them an aroused suggestion of more to come. By tacit agreement, they began to arrive earlier, sometimes as early as two hours before the clinic's scheduled opening for the day.

Lauren wondered why Luis had begun to leave so early each morning. She asked him about it, but he was vague, mentioning something about making early rounds at one of the hospitals where was on staff. It didn't even occur to Lauren to doubt Luis's explanation. She trusted him implicitly. They were a loving family, a vested one; in this she felt secure.

These early morning meetings went on for well over six months before either Patricia or Luis admitted to themselves or each other that they were more than just coffee and conversation between coworkers. It wasn't until a medical convention which they both attended in a distant city that they became lovers.

They had arranged to have adjoining rooms. The connecting door between the rooms remained unlocked, again by tacit agreement. That first night, they merely consummated what had been building between them for months now. Afterwards, they talked into the wee hours, expressing feelings and thoughts, emotions which both had felt but had previously left unsaid. Neither mentions *the fact that Luis is a married man with a family.*

Now Luis began withdrawing from Lauren, making excuses, using his professional responsibilities as justification, as an avoidance/delay tactic. There always seemed to be a reason why he couldn't come home directly, or why he'd be delayed.

"You go and take the kids, I just can't take the time off right now," Luis urged when Lauren approached him about a trip to Disney World the two of them had promised Lisa and Laurence. "Ask your mom to go with you and the kids. You know how she dotes on them. She'd probably love to go along," he tells Lauren.

"I'm sure she would love to go," Lauren replies, "but we don't want to go without you; we'll wait. When do you think you'll be able to get away?" she asks.

"I have no idea. We're swamped," he says. "Illness never takes a vacation." She lets the subject of vacation drop, for a time.

Several months later, as Lisa's Thanksgiving vacation is nearing, Lauren approaches Luis again about the trip to Disney World. This time she is more insistent. "Luis," she says, "we haven't had a vacation is nearly two years now. And you definitely deserve a break. You've been putting in a lot of long hours. This could be just the break you need."

But the break Luis wants is one that does not include Lauren and the kids. By this time he has also promised Patricia that the two of them will get away, attend a medical convention scheduled to take place in November. If he can convince Lauren to take the kids on to Disney World without him, this will be ideal, he feels.

"I have a suggestion," he says. "You guys go on to Disney World. You definitely deserve a vacation. I'll try to reschedule my patients or get the other partners to make room for them in their schedules. Let me call and make reservations for you guys right now." And he does, but he has no intention of joining them. And he doesn't.

After Lauren and the kids leave, Luis and Patricia finalize their convention plans. Luis will leave the following morning. He calls Lauren to tell her that he belatedly remembers that he is one of the featured speakers at the November convention, and for that reason, he cannot miss it. "I'm sorry, but it just can't be helped. Apologize to the kids for me; tell them I'll make it up to them," he adds guiltily.

Lauren doesn't know what to think, but she does know her husband, and she knows him well. Luis would never forget a speech that he is scheduled to make. In fact, he would have written the speech weeks earlier. He would have asked her to proof and type the speech for him, and he would have practiced it, repeatedly, with her and the kids as his audience. Luis is not a good speaker, but
he does okay with adequate preparation and practice. He is well aware of this fact, and so is Lauren.

For the remainder of the Disney trip, Lauren is deeply troubled. Laurence, who is now four, is almost hit by a car as the three of them cross a busy intersection because Lauren, who is usually so attentive to the kids, is now troubled and preoccupied. She has allowed Laurence to wander farther away from her than she ever would have under normal conditions.

She decides to cut their trip short, realizing that she isn't enjoying herself, and that the kids can't be having a good time of it either with her nerves as frayed as they are since Luis's call. They return home three days earlier than scheduled. She asks her mother to come over and stay with the kids. "I'm going to Seattle for the last few days of the convention. Maybe I can convince Luis to take a couple of extra days for just the two of us. We're long overdue for some quality time alone together," she tells her mother. Her mother readily agrees. She is glad to have her only grand children to herself for a few days. She loves spending time with them and spoiling them. They are such sweet, well-behaved children.

It is after midnight when Lauren arrives in Seattle, and by the time she has retrieved her luggage, she has decided not to call Luis, whom she figures is bound to be sound asleep by this time. *I'll just ease into bed and surprise him*, she tells herself. She feels positively euphoric just thinking about how lovely it will be to have a few nights alone with her husband.

At the desk, Lauren tells the sleepy attendant that her husband, in Room 1101, is expecting her. He asks to see her identification, ascertains that she is who she claims to be, and gives her the room key, a computerized card.

Unsuspecting, Lauren opens the door and finds Luis asleep, with Patricia in his arms. She becomes physically ill and would have fled the room, except she rushes into the bathroom to keep from throwing up all over the carpet. The commotion awakens Luis and Patricia, *but it is Lauren who gets the rude awakening.*

Now that their divorce is in progress, Luis and Patricia are dating openly, though Luis has begun to feel awkward around the other partners. Lauren and the children are changed people. Lisa's teachers wonder what happened to the precocious, twelve-year-old girl to cause such drastic changes in her behavior and attitude.

Laurence, who is now five, is becoming increasingly aggressive, constantly hitting, scratching, or biting his playmates. Lauren is too deeply depressed to deal effectively with Lisa and Laurence who have changed, seemingly overnight, from happy, cooperative, eager-to-please children to obstinate, aggressive, hostile ones. *The yield,* was it worth it?

Megan, Randy, and Gretel

Randy joined the air force right before he and Megan met. They corresponded regularly for almost a year, so when he went home on furlough for the first time since their initial meeting, they dated almost every night. Sometimes he'd even pick her up from work during her lunch hour, they'd lunch together, he'd take her back to work, and then he'd see her that evening after she got off from work. If they didn't go out, he'd invite her over to his place, or she'd invite him over to her place. The thirty days seemingly had wings, and in no time at all Randy was saying goodbye.

When Randy returned to his base assignment, he couldn't stop thinking about Megan. He wrote and asked her to come to California; they would live together. He really missed her, his letter said. She refused. He wrote back and asked her to marry him. "Being here without you is torture. It's so beautiful here, but I can't even really appreciate it for missing you," he told her in his next letter. "Come share it with me."

She wrote that they didn't know one another well enough to consider marriage. He wrote back, "I know you as well as I need to know you. I know I don't want to be here without you. Come to me. Marry me, please!"

They continued to correspond for another several months, then Randy wrote that he had received orders for an overseas assignment; that he'd be based in Germany. He again asked Megan to become his wife.

This time she wrote back that she would marry him, but that she wanted him to come home for the ceremony so that they could share it with family and friends.

Before shipping out to Germany, Randy requested and was granted thirty days of leave. He wrote and told Megan to go ahead with plans for the wedding, that they could use some of his brief leave time for their honeymoon before he'd have to leave for Germany.

They were married on a beautiful, April evening, only three days after Randy's arrival. They left immediately following the ceremony for their honeymoon, ever conscious of the short time remaining before oceans would be separating them. The honeymoon is brief, romantic and all the more sweet because of its brevity, but each is aware of the need to save some of Randy's leave time for moving their things from each of their bachelor apartments; they plan to sell duplicate items they will no longer need as a couple. They have decided to store the things they want to keep until they are ready to begin their married life stateside.

Megan drives Randy to the airport. Both are tearful as they say their farewells, saying how much they will miss each other and how much they hate to be separating so soon after saying their vows. Though both knew to expect this separation, it is so much harder than either could have possibly imagined. After Randy leaves, Megan cries for several hours; she wonders how she'll survive until they can be together again.

The following morning, Megan makes application for her passport. She also makes application for her military identification card.

She goes to a nearby Air Force Base to make the latter application. The application clerk requests verification that she is a recent, military dependent. She has not yet received the official copy of their marriage license. The clerk tells her that she must return after she has received the official papers which Randy will send to her from Germany.

Megan drives to work late, thinking about Randy and their brief honeymoon and about how much she wants to be with him. *I'll give notice today at work. I can't wait to get to Germany,* she says to herself.

Several weeks later, Megan returns to the base with the required verification to receive her military dependent identification card. By this time she has already gotten her passport as well as the necessary immunizations for a trip abroad. With military dependent identification, she is hoping to take advantage of discounts available to military personnel and their dependents when she buys her ticket to join her husband in Germany.

As she arrives back at her apartment, she can see the mail truck turning onto her street. She waits until her mail has been deposited before exiting the car. She is hoping for a letter from Randy, and she is not disappointed. But the news is not welcomed. In part, this is what he has written: *So you see, it would be senseless for us to spend all that money for you to come here now. It seems that my tour here might be much shorter than the customary two years, maybe even as short as six months. At this point I'm just not certain, but I'll keep you informed. As soon as I know something definite, I'll let you know.*

Megan is astounded. This is the first she has heard about a change of plans. She has wondered why his letters are so infrequent and brief. She remembers the constant flow of letters from California before they married, but she knows that he's in a foreign country now, and she doesn't know anything about the flow of mail from Germany. She doesn't even know if every letter that he's written has reached her. But she does know that she wants to be with Randy, if it's only for one month, one *night* even; she is certain that he wants the same thing. *I know he does,* she tells herself.

But during Randy's first week in Germany, he has met and gotten involved with a German girl named Gretel who is now almost two months pregnant with his child. Many of the people there think that she is his wife.

Megan has a friend, Cora, an older woman in whom she confides. When she shares what she has learned with Cora, who is quite cynical, Cora advises her, "Check him out, Honey. I know men. He's probably already shacked up with one of those German mamas."

Meanwhile, Megan writes to Randy. She also tries to call him at the barracks, but is told that he is no longer staying there. Now she begins to wonder if he has already been reassigned elsewhere. *Maybe I shouldn't send the letter*, she begins to think. *Maybe I should just wait to hear from him.*

Megan has a friend, Cora, an older woman in whom she confides. When she shares what she has learned with Cora, Cora, who is quite cynical, advises her, "Check him out, honey. I know men. He's probably already shacked up with one of those German mamas!"

"Cora, how can you say that?" Megan asks. "You know we're practically newlyweds. We're in love. You shouldn't be such a cynic."

"Honey," Cora responds, "if you knew men like I know men, you'd know that trusting one implicitly is just asking for pain; heartache. I'm not telling you not to love him, but what I am telling you is if you love him, love him with the understanding that he's weak and that being newlywed doesn't mean that he won't shack up with some other woman if you're unavailable, and even if you are, if he thinks he can get away with it. I know it's hard, but it's a hard truth that most women are compelled to come to grips with sooner or later."

"I do love him, Cora, and I know he loves me too. Maybe he's right. Maybe it would be a waste of money to go over there for such a short time," she says.

"A waste of whose money? If my memory serves me right, you've been talking about taking a well-deserved vacation for years now, even before you got married. It's your money. Use it for what you want. You've got your shots; you've got your passport; now go buy your ticket. Go for a two-week vacation, if nothing else. Plenty people from the United States vacation in Germany everyday. Check things out for yourself," Cora says.

Megan decides to take Cora's advice. She has already given notice at her job. There's no reason for her to stay. She buys her ticket through an agent who is able to get her a group rate. He also supplies her with an itinerary which she plans to use only if Randy has already been reassigned by the time she reaches his base.

Seven weeks and three days later, Megan arrives in Germany. She is exhausted but exhilarated. As soon as she checks into her hotel and unloads her baggage, she hires a taxi to take her to the barracks at Randy's base. Although she was told when she called from the states that he was not living at the base currently, it is the only address she has for him and she is hoping to get his new address from someone there. *Surely he left a forwarding address at the base. That's probably required,* she says to herself.

She hands the index card containing the address to the driver. As he drives to the base, Megan is wondering why Randy did not write or call to give her his new address. *Perhaps he just got moved and he's been trying to reach me at home,* she tells herself.

At the barracks she goes to the front desk, identifies herself as Randy Holmes's wife and asks for him. The desk clerk tells her to wait for a minute.

"Let me check our computer records," he says. But he already knows that Randy has moved out. He also knows that Randy is living with a

German woman whom he had assumed was Randy's wife. The clerk returns looking somewhat baffled. He hands Megan an index card with Randy's address on it. The clerk knows Randy socially, so he is wondering if he should try to reach Randy to let him know that an attractive, Black American woman who identifies herself as his wife is looking for him. He decides to mind his own business. *It's none of my concern,* he tells himself.

Megan has asked the taxi driver to wait. She gets back into the taxi and gives the index card containing the address to the driver. As he drives toward the base, Megan is wondering why Randy did not write or call to give her his new address. *Perhaps he just got moved and has been trying to reach me at home,* she thinks fleetingly. *But I couldn't reach him at the barracks several weeks ago,* she suddenly recalls.

After much too fast driving, sudden stops, and peering, Megan spots the address, pays the driver and exits the taxi. When she knocks, Gretel answers the door. "I'm looking for Randal Holmes," Megan says to Gretel. "Does he live here?" she asks.

Gretel understands very little English, but she comprehends that this attractive, Black, American woman is looking for, asking about, *her* Randy. She is attempting to respond when Randy arrives. At first he does not see Megan because he has come in the back door and Megan is still standing outside of the front door.

Gretel has not rearranged her body inside the doorway in order to permit Megan entrance. When Randy does spot her, he is at first disbelieving, then he begins to feel trapped between the two women. With a mixture of broken English and German, Gretel tries to ascertain who Megan is and exactly what her relationship is to Randy.

As Megan gets a clear view of the expression in Randy's eyes, she turns and flees. Again she has told the taxi driver to wait for her. She jumps into the taxi with tears streaming down her face. "Go, just go," she says, gesturing to the driver her desire for him to pull away quickly from the curb. She can see Randy attempting to follow her, and he is the *last* person on earth she wants to speak with at that moment.

Randy hails a cab and tells the driver to follow Megan's taxi. The taxi takes Megan back to her hotel. She pays the driver without waiting for change and goes into the hotel. She sits on a barstool, head hung low. Minutes later, Randy sits on the stool directly to her right. Megan is startled by his quietly spoken, "I'm so sorry." Steeped in misery, she hadn't even heard his approach. "I never meant this to happen. I love you. I want you. This happened because I was missing you so much. Can you, will you forgive me?" He pleads.

"Oh, Randy, how could you do this? We're still newlyweds. I've missed you too, but I didn't move in with some substitute or allow one to move in with me. You're obviously not the man I thought you were. I could never trust you now. Don't you know that?"

"You can trust me. I'll *never* do anything like this again," he says.

"Not to *me,* you won't. I'm not going to give you another chance to do it again to me." She tells him.

Randy can see that complete cognizance has dawned in Megan's eyes. Stunned by her presence, he is totally speechless now. Megan, too, is momentarily without speech. She is incredulous. Her heart wants to reject what her intellect instantly recognizes. *The Yield,* was it worth it?

Chapter IX

Donna, Neil, and Mannin

Donna, twice divorced mother of two adult sons, vowed she'd never marry again. Her first husband, Dale, the father of her sons, was an okay guy, but he wouldn't work steadily. During the course of the six years in which they were married, Dale quit or was fired from a total of seventeen jobs, and these are just the ones that Donna knew about. *There were others.*

Donna, who had recently completed law school when she and Dale got married, was trying to care for two baby boys, born *only eleven months apart*, and to study for the bar, and all of this in a crowded, unairconditioned apartment which they could barely afford because of Dale's erratic work habits.

Neil, Donna's second husband, was great during the two years in which they dated. As a licensed plumber, he kept Donna's plumbing in tip-top condition; he was good with the boys; he was always attentive to Donna's needs. If Donna so much as mentioned something that she wanted or something that the boys needed within Neil's hearing, *it was done*. Her protestations that it wasn't expected or that he was doing too much went unheeded. He'd shrug them off until the next time, then he'd do the same thing all over again. It was as if he anticipated opportunities to do things for her and the boys, as if he felt privileged to be the one to provide for their needs and wants. He couldn't seem to do enough for them. By the time he asked Donna to become his wife, and the boys to be his sons, she couldn't imagine their lives without him.

During the first few months of their marriage, life seemed idyllic. Donna began to practice with a small, local firm. The boys were doing well in school; Neil's business was thriving. As time passed, however, it was becoming increasingly obvious that Neil was an insecure man. Whenever Donna had to work late, he'd complain. To please him, she began to bring the work home rather than stay late to complete it. He then complained about her inattentiveness to him.

To Donna, this was a whole, new side of Neil, *one she hadn't known existed;* one she didn't care for at all. Prior to the marriage, whatever had pleased her had pleased Neil, or so he said. But within the first eighteen months of their marriage, Neil had done a complete about face, a three-hundred-sixty degree turn around. Where before the marriage, he had been pleasant, agreeable and attentive, he was now complaining, disagreeable and neglectful. One day when Donna asked him to fix a leak under the kitchen sink, he grumbled rudely, saying that he fixed leaky sinks all day, couldn't she give him a break once he got home. "Unlike you, I don't enjoy bringing my work home," he told her sarcastically. Where before the marriage Neil had often taken Donna and the boys out to dinner or ordered take-out and took it over to share with them, teasingly saying that he did so because "The love of my life is a lawyer, not a cook," he now complained constantly about her being a lousy cook. If she or one of the boys suggested they eat out, he griped about the expense. If Donna said she'd pay, he accused her of being a show-off, saying she was trying to belittle his profession, let the boys know that she made more than he.

By their fifth wedding anniversary, Donna had gotten fed up with the constant complaints, the on-going discord. For the approaching fall school term, she enrolled both the boys in a nearby boarding school where she could pick them up on weekends, got them settled, and told Neil that she wanted a divorce, vowing she'd never remarry.

During the course of the next ten years Donna dated occasionally, but never seriously. She devoted herself to raising her boys and becoming prominent in her profession. By her forty-seventh birthday, she had become partner in her law firm; the firm had recently hired another clerk, thirty-two year old Mannin Wexler.

Mannin had completed a tour in the navy before beginning law school, so at thirty-two he was still relatively new to the profession. He had no serious, personal commitments; he was ambitious. He was referred to as *a hunk* by many of the women who worked in the office building that housed the law firm.

When Mannin first saw Donna, he had no idea that she was fifteen years his senior. She looked thirtyish, slim; attractive. He was formally introduced to her, along with the other partners, shortly after he began clerking at the firm.

When he first approached her for a date, Donna laughed and said, "Mannin, I'm almost fifty years old; I have a son who is almost as old as you are. I'm not interested in dating anyone your age; in fact, I'm not interested in dating. *Period.*"

In response Neil says, "Donna, I'll admit you don't look like you eat, but you're bound to eat sometimes. What is the harm in allowing this struggling attorney to share a meal with you?" Laughing, Donna turned away.

The second time he approached her, he waited until she was leaving work for the day. He caught up with her as she was getting into her car. "Attorney Upshaw," he says, "these two tickets to the Aretha Franklin concert, front row seats, will go unused if you say no to me. How about it?"

Donna loves Aretha; she has everything Aretha has recorded. Mannin knows this; he's asked around. "Okay, I'll go, but it's no date. I told you, I'm *not* interested in dating. I'll meet you at the coliseum." He really wanted to pick her up, but he didn't argue. *At least she's going*, he reasoned.

Aretha was fabulous; they had a great time. After the concert, Mannin invited her out for a bite to eat, but she declined, telling him, "Women my age can't afford to eat this late at night. I'll see you in the morning." All the way home she hummed Aretha's latest hit; she felt *good.*

Before she could leave for work the following morning, the phone rings. "Have breakfast with me," Mannin pleads. "I had such a great time with you at the concert. I can't stop thinking about you."

"Mannin," she says, "I *never* eat breakfast. Why are you doing this? There must be hundreds of young women out there who would kill to go out with you. I've told you, I'm fifty years old."

"You're forty-seven. And so what? You know what they say, 'Age ain't nothing but a thang,' anyhow, I'm not interested in hundreds of women. It's you I want. And allow me to ask you the same question: why are you doing this? Can't you see you're driving me nuts!"

Mannin continues to pursue Donna; she continues to resist, for over a year, hoping he'll eventually lose interest and seek someone closer to his own age. But it doesn't happen. *He never lets up.* Not a week goes by that he doesn't ask her to go out with him, or to allow him to come over and *just talk.*

Finally she agrees to go out to dinner with him, then it is a movie, then another concert. This time it is Whitney Houston. They leave the concert in a very romantic mood. When he asks if he can come in for a nightcap, she relents. They have their nightcap, but before either of them can finish their drink, they are in each other's arms. They come together explosively. They fit like spandex; *they mesh* Mannin begins to urge Donna to marry him. He buys her a full karat diamond engagement ring. She refuses to take it, tells him, "I'm *too old* for you." But Mannin *will not* be denied. He is obsessed with her; he wants her for his wife, and he pursues her relentlessly. Finally, *she agrees.*

They become husband and wife on a beautiful, summer morning in August. Both her sons, and everyone at the law firm attend the brief ceremony. One of the partners performs it. Mannin is *exultant*! He has *his* Donna. He has won!

Because of their caseloads, they delay the honeymoon, the formal one that is, but life together for them is a honeymoon. They drive to work together each morning and home together at each day's end. As soon as the door closes behind them in the evening, they are tearing at their clothes, at one another's. They can't seem to get enough of each other.

One morning Mannin leaves home around six o'clock. He has done this with escalating frequency. Donna dresses hurriedly in her jogging clothes and drives to the building which houses Mannin's firm. His car is there in the parking lot, but the building is still dark, still locked. Feeling too despondent to begin the return drive, she sits with her head resting against the steering wheel, weary and unhappy. About forty-five minutes later, a bright yellow Mustang pulls into the lot, which is now beginning to fill. Donna can see Mannin on the passenger side in the in the Mustang. At the wheel is a red-headed woman. Mannin leans over and kisses the woman, long and lingeringly on the lips, then gets out and heads, whistling, for the building.

"Well, I'll be damned!" Donna hisses. She drives home slowly, as if she is in a daze. She calls her secretary and tells her that she will not be in to work that day. She calls Mannin and asks him to come home, saying only that she has an emergency.

When he arrives, she confronts him about what she has observed earlier that morning. She tells him that she has followed him on several occasions, so lying will be pointless, (although *this isn't so*). He admits that he is having an affair, says he needs some space, which is why he has left her firm; that he is feeling smothered.

Donna is divorcing Mannin. She feels forlorn, despondent; dispirited. She's trying to fathom why he pursued her so vigorously, finally got her, and then rejected her. She's having trouble getting a grip on that. It just doesn't make sense to her for him to have pursued her for more than a year and then, in less than a year, feel the need to have an affair.

She now goes about her daily life fulfilling her obligations, but the pleasure in life is truant.

Mannin, too, feels that something special has gone out of his life. He now has brief affairs with numerous women *looking for what he had*. He says he's trying to find the right woman. Was *the yield* worth it?

Gina, Alvin, and Infidelity

The first time Gina forgave Alvin and agreed not to leave him even though she knew he'd been unfaithful to her, he said he loved her and their girls, and he swore it would never happen again. After that though, she felt unable to trust him. Whenever he called to say he'd be delayed, for any reason, she'd wonder if he were telling the truth. Sometimes, for short periods, she'd almost forget about the betrayal, but the simplest thing would trigger a fresh wave of pain, a renewal of memory.

Gina reasoned: *he is the children's father; they do love and need him. He says it'll never happen again, but never again can I trust him unconditionally. In fact, I can never trust any man unconditionally again, but maybe in time, if it really doesn't happen again, I'll be able to close the door on it.*

When Gina and Alvin married, he worked for a major pharmaceutical company as a traveling salesman. He was on the road a good deal of the time during the first six years of the marriage. In fact, he was away on travel when the last two of their three girls were born. But by the time Nina, their eldest, was eleven, Alvin had worked his way up to district manager. At this level he made a good salary and traveled less. Throughout Alvin's travels, he has had a string of affairs, all of which he has managed to keep Gina ignorant of, except one.

As district manager, Alvin became a salaried employee. He no longer had to depend on commissions to support his family. The family moved into a nice home in an upscale neighborhood. All three of the girls are in private school and doing well. Of course Gina considers all of this when she makes the decision forgive Alvin and to keep the family unit intact. But she cannot forget that Alvin could have exposed himself and her, unknowingly, to any number of sexually transmitted diseases.

Two years have passed and the family is doing fine. Alvin has doubled his efforts to be discreet, though he *has not stopped* the philandering. Then, seemingly out of nowhere, the phone begins to ring late at night. The phone in the master suite is on Gina's side of the bed, so she is always the one who answers it when they are in bed. When she answers these late night calls, there is no response. At first she thinks it is just someone dialing the wrong number, but as time passes and it continues, always late at night, she begins to suspect that something is amiss.

She lets it ring one late night until Alvin answers it. She has deliberately avoided going to bed, hoping the phone will ring and that Alvin will be in the bedroom already. She has already flipped on the recorder and has fallen asleep on the sofa in the family room. She doesn't listen to the recording until the following morning, and this is what she hears: "Alvin, I'm not getting an abortion this time!" This is followed by a click, indicating a broken connection. A prerecorded message says the familiar spiel about, *If you'd like to make a call...*

By the time Gina listens to the message, Alvin has already left for work. As she calls the girls for their cereal, gets them off to school, and gets herself dressed for work, her emotions are in turmoil. All of the pain of the original betrayal resumes its vicious assault. *What does this mean?* she wonders. *Is this the same woman? Maybe he never broke it off. Maybe everything he told me was a lie; maybe he just told me it was over.* She has these thoughts as she prepares for the new day.

As Gina drives to work, she decides to confront Alvin as soon as he gets home from work.

She leaves work early enough to pick the girls up from their school. She has arranged with Bessi, her best friend who is between jobs at the moment, to keep the girls for her. She drops them there.

When Alvin arrives home, Gina plays the tape for him, tears streaming down her face. Alvin, on his knees, clasps Gina around the knees. "Please, Gina," he says. "Don't let this destroy our family. Our girls need both of us; you know they do. This is not important enough to fragment our family. That woman is lying. I don't know anything about any abortion. Maybe she has had one, but it has nothing to do with me," he says, *lying glibly.*

"Have you slept with her? Could it possibly be yours? What's her name?" Gina asks all of these questions, blowing her nose and drying her eyes intermittently. She moves out of Alvin's clasp and sits on the sofa. She puts her head down on the arm of the sofa, despising Alvin at the moment, refusing to look at him.

"Only once, I swear. And it'll never happen again. I've learned my lesson. Will you forgive me and help me to keep our family together?" he pleads. "You don't have to give me an answer right now. I'm leaving in the morning for that Charleston trip I told you about. I'll be gone for three days. Think about all I've said. Let me know your decision when I return. But please, please, Gina, don't let this break up our family, fragment our girls, and destroy our love. You know I love you and our girls.

Gina is thinking, *but he is the one destroying our love, impacting our family unity. And he could be abbreviating our lives as well, exposing us to all kinds of life-threatening diseases.*

How can Alvin be so shallow, so stupid, so weak that he would put his sex drive above the welfare and well-being of our girls? Our children do need both of us, but they could be deprived of both of us if we've been exposed to AIDS. How can Alvin discount that? I have obviously accredited him with more intelligence than he possesses.

During the course of the next three days, Alvin has a dozen, plus three beautiful red roses delivered to Gina at her job. The enclosed card reads: "These aren't nearly as beautiful as you and our girls. Give each of them a rose and a kiss from their daddy. I love all of you so much. Love Eternal, *Al.*"

All of the other women at the office *Ooh and aah,* and tell Gina how lucky she is to be married to a hunk who also happens to be romantic. Gina smiles past the lump in her throat, making no verbal response.

Later that evening, Alvin calls to say that he will be home the following day. He asks Gina if she and the girls will meet him at the airport. He makes no mention of the phone call exposing the infidelity; neither does she, though it has occupied her thoughts every waking moment since its occurrence.

The next evening when the plane arrives, Gina and the girls are there. The girls are always excited to see their dad, even when he hasn't been away, and even more so when he has. Alvin has a gift for each of them: sweatshirts for the girls and Gina's favorite perfume for her.

"Have you guys eaten yet?" Alvin asks. In chorus, the girls say no, anticipating what he will say next. "Why don't we stop somewhere for dinner?" he asks. "All they served on the plane were peanuts, and you know how I hate peanuts."

"Yuk!" the girls all say in unison. *If Alvin doesn't like it, then it isn't worth eating.*

"Why don't we stop somewhere for dinner?" he asks. The girls argue loudly for a few minutes. Finally they agree on a favorite spot.

As they sit down to eat, the girls' lively chatter sheathes the awkwardness between Alvin and Gina. Several times during the meal their eyes lock, transmitting some silent, esoteric message. Each is wondering what the other is thinking.

During the three days that Alvin was gone, Gina had been unable to come to a decision, at least not to a final one. Initially she decided that it would be best to leave while the girls were still young enough to cope, hopefully, less traumatically. Then she changed her mind; then she changed back it again.

Now she is thinking: *how can I do this to them? They love him so much. Their eyes are sparkling just because he's near. They have no idea that he is even capable of putting their happiness at risk. He is much of the source of their happiness. We, the two of us, are their whole world. How can I willingly play a part in its disintegration?*

The girls are now asleep in bed. Alvin has told them about his trip, which they always insist upon when he returns from one. He has read them a bedtime story. They have fallen asleep happy, secure; contented. As he leaves their room, he stops by the fridge and pours two glasses of champagne. He has put it in the freezer before heading for the girls' room.

He takes them with him into the master suite. As he enters, Gina is lying, fully clothed, across the bed, leafing listlessly through a magazine, *Redbook*. Her eyes are on the page, but she sees nothing. She is preoccupied with indecision.

Alvin sets one of the glasses on the nightstand on Gina's side of the bed, then he says, "I can see you're undecided. I know I don't deserve you and our beautiful daughters, but please, let me hold you for just a little while. I've ached to hold you ever since I left for Charleston." As he is saying this, he lies down next to her and takes her into his arms. He crushes her to him with tears in his eyes, in his voice. She, too, is crying, heart-wrenching sobs of acquiescence.

Her mind tells her to *say no; that he can't be trusted*, but her heart shouts, moans, *Yes*! Alvin begins to caress her in all the places he knows she likes to be touched: behind her ears, her lips, her neck; her breasts. Slowly, he undresses her.

Momentarily, she is able to close the curtain, to lose herself in their shared passion. Fleetingly, Alvin thinks*: everything is okay; she has forgiven me.*

Another year (eleven months actually) has gone by. Things have been going smoothly for them and the family is progressing nicely. It is now the Christmas season. Alvin, just returning from his final trip until after the new year, is unloading his bags. Gina joins him, helping to unload the gifts which he has brought back for the girls, before they discover that he is home. As she removes the last two wrapped gifts from the bag, a package of condoms is wedged between them; it falls to the floor. They bend, simultaneously, to retrieve it, Alvin hoping to conceal; Gina hoping to verify. Gina reaches it first;

she and Alvin's eyes lock.

At just that moment the girls pile into the room with delighted cries of "Daddy, Daddy." They begin chattering all at once. Hina, the youngest, runs and jumps into Alvin's arms, asking, "Dad, what did you bring me?" The other two girls each grab a leg.

Gina leaves the room, allowing the girls to greet their dad, and herself a few minutes to regain a modicum of composure. She goes into the kitchen and sits at the table, head in hands. Her joy in the approaching holiday has vanished.

For the first time in fifteen years of marriage Gina does not accompany Alvin to his parents' home for Christmas dinner. "You go and take the girls," she tells him. "I'm not going this year."

"But what'll I tell Mom and Dad?" he asks.

"Why don't you tell them about the condoms, Alvin, the ones you and I have no need for? she says. "I don't care what you tell them. I just know that I can't go there, eat, drink, and be merry, and pretend all is well. So you decide what you want them to know, and *that's* what you tell them," she concludes.

Alvin and the girls depart for the two-hour drive early on Christmas morning.

Gina feigns sleep as they depart. She is not up to answering the girls' questions about why she isn't going with them to Gramma's and Papa's house for dinner.

The depth of her despair is infinite. She literally cannot rise from her bed. She tries, in vain, to make her mind go blank so that she can get a few hours of sleep.

She hasn't slept all night.

I can't go on like this, she tells herself. *If I do, I'll die, and my girls need me. I might die anyhow. I have no idea to what I've been exposed. I'm so sorry I didn't leave Alvin that first time. All of this could have been long past, and maybe the girls would have adjusted all right. I knew he couldn't be trusted, and like a fool, I hoped; I trusted him anyhow!*

Resolutely, Gina gets up. It takes every ounce of her strength. She feels feeble, drained. Her legs actually wobble and she has to clasp the bedpost to steady herself. She goes first to the girls' room and packs a bag for each of them. She next returns to her and Alvin's suite and packs a bag for herself. Next she gets dressed.

Finally, she gets everything loaded into the station wagon. She wishes she had the van, but it is the newer of their two cars and Alvin took it for the trip to his parents' house. She drives to a local hotel, rents a double room for three days, and unloads the bags.

Both of Gina's parents are dead. She was reared in a series of foster homes, so she wants her girls to grow up in a home where they are secure and loved, and even a little spoiled. As she sits in the rented room thinking about this, tears spill down cheeks. She is also thinking that Alvin will not, perhaps cannot, help her to provide these things for her girls. *You have to love yourself before you can really love someone else,* she tells herself. *How can Alvin love himself if he willingly exposes himself to life-threatening diseases? He simply cannot be trusted. What he wants is obviously the prerequisite for the choices he makes. The children and I will always be secondary to his sexual appetite. I know that now. But my girls don't know that, and maybe I should go back for their sakes and try to live with that knowledge without exposing the girls to it. Maybe I should take the chance that they'll never have to know it. I owe them the chance to grow up with both their parents the chance that I didn't have. There were times when I would have done anything to have my own parents raising me. Well, now I've got the chance to give that to my girls. No sacrifice is too great for them!*

As Gina is thinking this, she gets up and begins to put the bags back into the station wagon. She has to make six trips to accomplish the task and is crying so hard that she has to stop intermittently to blow her nose and dry her eyes. As she reloads the final bag she is thinking, contrasting this sad, depressing time with happier holidays of the past: *she and Alvin and the girls gathered around the tree, with Hina on his shoulders trying to put the angel atop; the five of them driving home from Gramma and Papa's singing carols offkey; she and Alvin being awakened on Christmas morning, much too early, by all three of the girls piling onto their bed at once. Her mind registers the girls in the snow with Alvin, building a snowman; the five of them having a snowball fight; Alvin sledding with the girls screaming all the way downhill...*

As she drives back to the house, she is thinking about the love and respect, the reverence she once had for Alvin, which is now a thing of the past. *She remembers how her heart once gladdened at the sound of his voice, how everything was right with her world when she, and Alvin, and the girls were together safe, secure; warm.*

Gina now lives for her girls. She prays for the day when they will no longer need a mother and a father to feel secure and loved. But the affection, the desire for Alvin's touch, the richness of the union are lost, perhaps forever. The light that once brightened her eyes and gladdened her heart at the sound of his voice has been extinguished. *The yield*, was it worth it?

Renee, Earl, Juanita

Earl and Renee have been married for thirteen years. They have no children. They both agreed from the first that neither wanted children; that they wanted to be able to devote all of their time to pleasing each other.

Renee was an only child, and even though from time to time she thought it might be nice to have a child, she is not overly fond of children. They tend to be messy; she likes having a place for everything and everything in its place.

As a legal secretary for a large, successful firm, she likes the freedom having no kids afford her. While coworkers rush out of the door at exactly five o'clock to pick up their children, or leave work unexpectedly for kid-related emergencies, she relaxes. After work she and Earl frequently meet for dinner or for drinks. Sometimes he calls her and says, "Meet me at home directly after work; it's urgent! She knows exactly what that means. She loves being able to devote herself and her time to their relationship.

Earl has two brothers; no sisters. He also enjoys their life together. Both of his brothers have kids, and while he enjoys being an uncle, he also likes knowing that at the end of each day when he goes home, he won't have to wait until kids have been fed, and rocked, and indulged before he can indulge himself. As a high-powered criminal lawyer, he feels the need to use his sparse, leisure time for himself. He is glad, thankful even, for an attractive, loving wife who shares these feelings with him.

Earl and Renee had met for the first time when he was a third-year law student. He had interned the summer preceding his third year at the firm where she works as a legal secretary. During that summer, they had dated a few times, but not seriously.

Almost four years later, they bumped into one another at the supermarket. By this time Earl has graduated and has already passed the bar. He is now partner in a small, but lucrative law firm with two other attorneys, buddies from law school: Mark and Jesse. He and Renee can't get over running into one another like that. They feel like old friends. This happened during the Christmas season and Renee invites Earl to her office party which is scheduled the following Friday, three days away. Earl graciously accepts, saying how good it is to see her and how much he is looking forward to renewing their acquaintance.

The *office party* turns out to be an enormous, semi-formal affair held in the grand ballroom of the downtown Ritz Carlton. They have a good time, but leave after three hours, anxious to be alone to talk, to catch up on what has been happening in each of their lives since they last saw one another. They go to an all-night diner, take a private booth, and talk until almost 3A.M. When he finally, reluctantly takes her home, they have agreed to meet for dinner the following evening.

Dinner turns out to be another marathon talk session. Again it is close to 3A.M when they reluctantly separate, but not before making a date for the following evening. This time Earl has invited her to his townhouse for dinner, an extravagant, catered affair for two.

Because they both work in the law profession, they can talk forever and never run out of things to say to each other it seems. They mesh in other ways too. In fact, both have already decided, before either voices it, that they are meant for each other.

When Earl asks Renee to become his wife, she has already decided that she will ask him if he doesn't ask her soon. She can't say yes quickly enough. Neither of them wants to wait in order to plan a large wedding. They are wed in a small, civil ceremony only three weeks later. The wedding reception is an enormous, fabulous affair, held in the same Ritz Carlton Ballroom where they feel they fell in love. Many of their friends, family members and coworkers are there to celebrate with them. They both feel the birth of something grand, and they are immensely pleased with themselves and with each other too. The smiles on their faces extend directly into their hearts. They are intoxicated, and the champagne, still in their glasses, except for diminutive sips which they took to toast their happiness, does not contribute.

During the immediate three weeks prior to the marriage, they have looked at several houses and have found the perfect place. It is spacious; they both like to entertain. It is somewhat isolated; they like their privacy.

Following the honeymoon, they move into their house. For most of that first year of their marriage, they frequent estate sales looking for just the right pieces. They furnish the master suite first, putting odds and ends from each of their bachelor places in the other rooms. But when the master suite is flawless, they start on the other rooms. They take their time doing them, concentrating on one at a time. They shop together, often meeting after work to hunt for furniture or to look at some piece one or the other has learned about through a coworker or a salespaper. By the end of that first year, the house, which reflects their mutual taste, is complete. And it is gorgeous; tasteful with unstated elegance. They are tickled pink with their accomplishment. Sometimes they stand, arms linked, in a doorway of one room or another, and grin like two kids. Both are still in the honeymoon mode. Life continues happily, contentedly, for the Braxtons. Among their friends they are a favored couple, always being invited to parties, receptions, weekend jaunts. They accept or decline, depending on their mutual plans. They can scarcely believe that they are looking forward to celebrating their thirteenth wedding anniversary. They prefer to celebrate their anniversary privately. This time, however, friends have planned a surprise celebration for them. They leave home believing that just the two of them have been invited to supper by another couple, mutual friends with whom they go out occasionally: Juan and Stephanie. But Juan and Stephanie have also invited five other couples and the supper has been planned in honor of their thirteenth wedding anniversary. The only single person there is Juan's twin sister, Juanita, and she wasn't actually invited. Unaware of the celebration, she dropped by for an unannounced visit and they put her to work making salad.

Supper turns out to be a five-course meal. Everyone enjoys the delectable food and the camaraderie, but by eight o'clock, the party is beginning to break up; tomorrow is a workday for each of them.

All of the coats have been piled onto a bed in one of the guest bedrooms Stephanie has asked Juanita to assist the guests with the retrieval of their coats As Earl enters the bedroom and reaches for his and Renee's coats, Juanita plants a playful kiss on his lips, chuckling as she does so. "Watch it, girl," Stephanie says, coming through the door into the bedroom. "That man is already spoken for."

Juanita, who is quite flirtatious, had meant the kiss innocently enough, but during the brief contact, she feels a definite attraction. *Umm, I wonder if he felt it too,* she ponders fleetingly as Earl gets the coats and exits the bedroom.

After that occurrence, whenever Juanita sees Earl or Renee, she remembers that kiss. She often finds herself daydreaming about what a *real* kiss from Earl would be like. *I'd sure like to find out,* she says to herself.

Several months later, Juanita sees Earl going into a health spa. She pulls into the lot and parks her car, a red convertible. She goes into the health club and looks around for Earl, but doesn't see him. She asks one of the attendants to show her around and to tell her about the services offered by the spa. As the attendant does so, she barely listens to the sales pitch, constantly looking around in an effort to spot Earl. As they enter the weight room and the attendant begins to talk about the equipment there, Juanita sees Earl. Pretending to be surprised to encounter him there she says, "I didn't know you were a member here too!" The attendant gives Juanita a puzzled glance, but says nothing. Earl smiles, shakes his head affirmatively, and continues to pump iron. When Earl makes no verbal response, the attendant continues the sales pitch. As soon as they move out of his hearing range, Juanita interrupts again with, "How much is a trial membership?"

She takes her time filling out the trial membership application. As she does so, she continues to glance up intermittently to assure that Earl does not leave without her awareness. By the time she has completed the application, Earl has showered, changed, and is heading for the exit. "Can I get a ride?" Juanita asks, falling in step with him. "My car won't crank," she says, lying.

"Sure," Earl responds. "Where to? He asks.

In the car Juanita says, "I'm starving. I skipped breakfast, and now this! I was intending to stop for a sandwich and a drink. Earl says that he's hungry too, that he always waits until after he works out to eat, and then he's usually ravenous. As they eat, Juanita elicits Earl's promise to drop her off at her apartment, which is a twenty-minute drive outside of the city. When they arrive there, she invites him in for coffee saying, "I put the pot on before I left, expecting to be gone only for a short time, so it's already brewed."

"Okay, but it'll have to be fast," he says as they exit the car. Inside the apartment, Juanita puts a C.D. on, barely audible, and then goes into the kitchen. She quickly heats two cups of water in the microwave and stirs in instant coffee.

"Make yourself at home," she calls to Earl as she puts cream and sugar containers onto a tray, along with the cups of coffee. She takes the tray into the living room. As they share the coffee, they stare into one another's eyes. They can feel something happening. Still maintaining eye contact Juanita sets her cup down and moves to stand between Earl's legs. She places her lips on his. They begin kissing, slowly, softly at first, then more urgently. Right there on the sofa they begin to undress themselves, each other.

Heading home, Earl can't believe he allowed himself to be unfaithful to his wife, his vows. He loves Renee; he loves their life together. He is torn between confessing and begging her forgiveness, and sparing her the pain of knowing he betrayed her; he chooses the later.

But Renee is not to be spared. Five weeks later Juanita calls Earl at his office; she tells him that she is pregnant with his child. "What're we going to do?" she asks. When Earls makes no response, she says, "My family is catholic, so don't even suggest abortion. It's no option for me."

That night Earl is too stressed out to sleep soundly, for the first time since he was studying for the bar, years ago. His unaccustomed tossing and turning awakens Renee. "Are you okay?" she asks.

Earl has promised Juanita that he'll get back to her, but he has not yet done so. He is busy juggling several cases, and he and Renee do spend all of their leisure time together. It has been like that for them from the first; it's the way they like it; also, he is reluctant to call Juanita because he doesn't know what to say to her; he doesn't know what she expects of him. He wishes he could turn back the clock and tell Juanita to find herself another ride home. He wishes he could forget all about their encounter. He wishes for the times when all he had to think about were his wife and his job, in that order. Recurrently, he finds himself staring into space, preoccupied, when he should be concentrating on his caseload.

Juanita waits for another week, but when she still has heard nothing from Earl, she calls him at his home. Luckily, he answers the phone. He rarely answers the phone at home, but Renee is in the shower. "Why haven't you called me?" Juanita asks, without preamble.

"I don't know what you want me to say, Juanita. I don't know what to say; that's why I haven't called. I'm sorry," he tells her.

"It's too late for *sorry,* Earl. What are we going to do?" He tells her that he doesn't know what to do. He asks what she wants him to do. "Get a divorce and marry me, that's what. You don't have any kids, so it shouldn't be too complicated," Juanita says.

"Let's get one thing straight," Earl says, as he cocks one ear, listening to be sure that the shower is still going. "I love my wife; I don't want a divorce. Just as abortion is no option for you, divorce is no option for me. Is that clear?"

Juanita digests this, she begins to get angry. She already doesn't like the fact that Earl didn't return her phone call, that she had to call him a second time. She thought he'd be excited, maybe, about the prospect of having a child, a son perhaps.

"What do *you* mean, divorce is not an option?" she asks angrily. "Of course divorce *is* an option; as I see it, it's the only viable option!" she concludes.

Still keeping an ear tuned toward the phone, Earl hears Renee as she turns off the water. Into the phone he says, "I'm sorry, I'll have to go now," and hangs up before Juanita has a chance to respond.

Coming out of the shower wrapped in a towel, Renee says, "I thought I heard the phone ring. Who was it?" Earl tells her that it was a wrong number.

Later, as Earl lies in bed, again too stressed out to sleep soundly, he is thinking: *tonight is the first time in thirteen years of marriage that I've lied to my wife about a phone call to our home. Renee isn't just my wife, she's also my best friend. God, how can I tell her this?*

Four months later, seething from no contact with Earl, Juanita calls Renee at work. "I need to talk with you," she says. "Can you meet me at noon today at that diner on the corner of First and Gerard?"

"What is this about, Juanita? I'm awfully busy. I usually work through lunch and just eat a piece of fruit at my desk," Renee tells her.

"I'd rather not get into it on the phone. Please, this won't take very long," she says in response. Renee agrees to meet her, but she tells her that she has only half an hour.

When Renee arrives at the diner, which is just across the street from where she works, Juanita is already there nursing a half-filled cup of lukewarm coffee. *She must have phoned me from here,* Renee realizes. Juanita is nervous, but determined. As soon as Renee sits down she says to her, "Renee, I'm almost five months pregnant."

"And? What has it to do with me?" Renee wants to know. Juanita tells her that Earl is the father of the child she is carrying. Renee feels as if Sugar Ray Leonard has punched her in the stomach. For a moment she is disoriented; totally disconnected from the restaurant, the setting. "That's a lie! My husband would never be unfaithful to me; he would never risk what we have."

But as she is saying this, she doesn't feel nearly as certain as she sounds. Her *awry circuit is* triggered. Some primitive instinct tells her that this woman would not have called her away from her job to tell her this if there were no truth to it. Renee now says, "You'd better find someone else to blame. I'm not buying this!" With that, she gets up and flounces out of the diner.

For the first time since Renee began her job as a legal secretary, nearly twenty years ago, she does not return to work after lunch. For the first time since their marriage, she calls Earl and asks him to come home when he takes his lunch hour. She knows that he usually takes his lunch hour at 2p.m. "I'm not feeling well," is the only explanation she offers. And she it totally truthful.

When Earl arrives home, Renee is in bed. She really does not feel well. She *is* sick, *heartsick*. Earl enters the bedroom concerned, solicitous. "What's the matter, baby?" he asks.

She looks up at him, eyes brimming with tears. Now he begins to feel fearful, thinking maybe she's learned that she has some dreaded disease. "What is it, Renee?" he asks. "You're scaring me," he says.

With tears streaming down her cheeks, she relates the conversation with Juanita. Before she is halfway through the story, she can see the misery, the desolation, in his eyes. She knows, before he utters a word, that it's all true. The pain that grips her at that moment is physical. Never has she felt such searing agony. Her trust in her husband was implicit; her belief in their oneness total. *Marriage*, they had often agreed, *is built on trust. When there is no trust, there is no real marriage.* Both of them understood that their love, their commitment, had deepened and developed character. It had become so much more than just satisfying sex and companionship. It had become their life. Neither had ever even contemplated their lives as separate entities, not once since the day they said, *I do*.

Earl begins to implore Renee to forgive him. "It happened just that one time," he says, "and I know it's inexcusable. I don't know what came over me, but I do know this: I love you with all my heart. I'd never, intentionally cause you pain."

Continuing to weep quietly, she says, "But it was intentional, Earl. She didn't rape you, did she? She didn't take you, at gunpoint, wherever it was that it happened, did she?" To this, Earl does not respond, but he reaches for her instead. For the first time in their marriage, she shuns his embrace. Just then she can't bear for him to touch her. All she is able to think of is *Earl with another woman.* Her pain is palpable, visible, almost tangible. There is nothing he wouldn't do to change it. But that is no longer his to control. When the control switch was his, he chose not to activate it. *The yield*, was it worth it?

Asa and Darryl

Asa and Darryl were in the army when they met. Asa joined the army right out of high school. She became interested in doing so when recruiters came to her high school to talk with juniors and seniors about how they could join the army and earn enough money in two years to attend college for four. At that time, Asa, a senior, lived with her alcoholic mother and whatever *uncle* just happened to be currently favored by her mother. Asa was accustomed to circumventing these uncles, and had become quite adroit at so doing. But she was looking forward to a time in her life when she could go to bed and rest easy, a time when she wouldn't have to be concerned with fighting off the unwanted advances of some unknown, undesirable and smelly old man.

Darryll had graduated from college. He had been in the R.O.T.C., and received his commission as an officer upon graduation. His dad is a retired army general; his mom a retired high school principal. He is their only son. He was reared with the best, and they have very high expectations for him.

When Asa first read about the assembly which had been scheduled for interested juniors and seniors, she stopped by her counselor's office to ask about a flyer she'd seen advertising it. The counselor tells her she'll have to attend the assembly to get the details, that army recruiters will be conducting the assembly, and that they will be talking about how money for college tuition and other expenses can be earned, saved, and matched, among other things.

Asa is definitely interested. She has been wondering how she can possibly get money to go to college. Somewhere, in back of her mind, she has always wanted to go. She can't really remember when she decided it, all she knows is that college has been a dream of hers since she first learned about it. She also knows that she can't count on getting any money for college from her mother, and she has no idea who her father is or where he is. From time to time she used to ask her mother about her father. At those times, her mother had always said that her father was long gone, that she has no idea where he is; that if he were interested in them, she imagined he wouldn't have too much trouble looking them up. Asa had stopped, years ago, trying to engage her mother in conversation about her father. It only makes her sad and angry. She used to daydream that her father loved her and would one day come and rescue her, but these daydreams had also stopped years ago. Asa has been aware, for years now, that if she is to be rescued, she'd better get about the business of rescuing herself.

Asa has a good friend, Tamika, whose parental situation is similar to her own. They have been best friends since fourth grade. They also look a lot alike, but that's where the similarity ends. Where Asa is astute and ambitious, Tamika is uninterested and apathetic; where Asa little interest in getting serious with boys, Tamika has had several serious relationships and is not happy unless she has a serious and steady boyfriend. They are both seniors, and were together when they stopped by the counselor's office. As they are leaving the office, Asa says to Tamika, "Let's go to that assembly. We could find out something that could positively impact our future."

"Positively what?" Tamika asks. "You go, Girl!" Tamika says laughingly.

"You know what I mean, Girl!" Asa says.

The two of them go to the assembly together. Tamika isn't really interested; she goes only because it gives her a legitimate excuse for missing class. During the assembly, she keeps talking to Asa who keeps saying,

"Shhh, I'm trying to hear."

Finally, Tamika gives up and sits, feeling bored. As soon as the assembly ends, Asa goes up to one of the recruiters and tells him, "I'm definitely interested." He talks to her for a few minutes, then he gives her a card and tells her to fill it out and leave it with her counselor. He tells her that the cards will be picked up from the counselors and that all interested juniors and seniors will be notified when the next meeting is scheduled.

About a week later, all of the seniors who filled out interest cards are invited to a second assembly. At this assembly, each senior is given an opportunity to talk, individually, with one of the recruiters. Each has already gotten the required parental signature, which is necessary for attendance at this second assembly for those students who are not yet eighteen.

Within a month of graduation, Asa is on her way to Fort Hood Army Base in Texas, for basic training. She completes basic with flying colors and is on her way home for a thirty-day leave period when she meets Darryll for the first time. He is the navigator on the plane. She is unaware of this at the time of their meeting; she knows only that he is very handsome and very polite. He is dressed in army attire, but she is in civilian dress, so she knows that he is an army officer, but Darryll is unaware that she is in the army.

There is an hour layover and Asa has to change planes. The two of them introduce themselves and learn that they are both headed for Chicago. After talking for a while, Darryll asks if she has a steady boyfriend. She says that she does not, so he asks if she'd like to go out on Saturday night. It is now a Thursday afternoon. "I'd love to go out on Saturday," she tells him, and gives him her home phone number.

That Saturday as Asa waits for Darryll to pick her up, she has dressed early and sits looking out the window. When she sees him approaching, she goes to the door and meets him, calling, "Good-bye, Mother," as the two of them depart. *I wonder, why she didn't invite me in to meet her mother,* is Darryll's fleeting thought. He knows that his parents would never have allowed his younger sister, Amelia, to go out with someone whom they had not met. He is thinking about this as he opens the door for Asa to get into the car.

Darryll takes Asa to dinner at a really terrific restaurant, *a first for her;* she tells him this. When she says, "I've never eaten at a place like this before; it's incredible." He reminds her that she'd told him she'd been raised right there in Chicago, and then he asks where did they eat when they ate out. In response she laughs and says, "McDonalds, where else?"

"We ate at McDonalds lots of times too, but on really special occasions, my family sometimes ate at really nice places, like this one," he says.

As the conversation continues, Asa learns just where in Chicago he had grown up; she learns the name of the private, catholic high school from which he graduated; that both of his parents are retired professionals. She tells him about herself; she even tells him about her mom's drinking problem, but she does not mention her dad.

She is ashamed to admit that she doesn't know who her dad is, has never even met, seen or heard from him. She also tells Darryll that she is in the army and that she joined the army to earn money for college. As she is talking, Darryll is thinking: *so that's why she didn't ask me in to introduce me to her mother.* He is also wondering why she didn't mention her father, but he's too polite to ask her why.

As Darryll is paying the check, a couple, Wayne and Mandy, stops by their table. Darryll grew up with the two of them; they are newlyweds. He introduces Asa to the two of them and they invite Darryll and Asa to stop by their place later in the evening for cocktails. Mandy says, "We're having two other couples over and would love it if you guys would join us."

Later that evening at the Wetherby's, Asa meets the two other couples. These are also people with whom Darryl has grown up, all except one of them, a young woman named Beth, who he is also meeting for the first time.

As the evening progresses into late night, Asa is thinking: *they're all so sophisticated and articulate. I'll bet I'm the only one here who hasn't gone to college. I'm probably also the only one here who doesn't know her father.* As Asa has these thoughts, there is a faraway look in her eyes. Darryll interrupts a conversation he is having with Wayne to ask, "Are you okay?" because of the expression on her face. She smiles sweetly and tells him that she is just fine.

It is close to midnight when they leave the Wetherby's, but Darryll is not ready to take Asa home. There is something about her that gets to him, something that sets off emotions in him with which he is not familiar, emotions that make him feel a bit confused, like a young boy on his first date. He can't decide exactly what it is, but as he talks with her, as he observed her as she talked with others at the Wetherby's townhouse, as he watches her with his peripheral vision while he drives, it's almost as if she is brooding. So he says to her, "Asa, my parents are visiting friends in the country this weekend. Come home with me. I'll make coffee and we can continue this conversation. I want to get to know you better. You intrigue me."

"Don't you have any brothers or sisters who might object to being disturbed this late at night," she asks. He tells her that he has no brothers; that he has one sister, but that she is away at school, so she isn't likely to object. She agrees to go, but for only a short time. "It's already after midnight," she reminds him.

As he approaches their house and pulls into the driveway, the garage door opens, as if by magic. Asa thinks fleetingly, *someone must be at home, and must've seen the car coming*, but she says nothing. As they pull into the garage and she sees no one, she realizes that she doesn't know exactly how the garage door opened, but she isn't about to ask.

He shows her around; she gazes in wonder at the splendor of the house. She has seen houses like this one in magazines and on television, but she has never known anyone who actually lived in a house like this. She has never been in one before. "Is this where you grew up?" she asks

"We moved here when I was nine, so I guess this is where I grew up," he responds. Her thoughts keep arching, like a roller coaster. She can't help contrasting this place with the string of Section Eight Apartments and low-rent row houses where she grew up. He saves his room for last, saying, "This is really where I grew up." He shows her his tape and C.D. collection, and exclaims when he realizes they both love the same music, the same artists.

"Put this one on," Asa says, when he pulls out a love ballad that Luther Vandross can croon like no one else in the world. The music begins to permeate every cell, every atom in the room: the walls, the carpet, the curtains; their bodies.

"May I have this dance?" he asks, as Luther pulsates and swells like a human heart working overtime. She goes into his arms like it is the most natural thing in the universe. By the time the song ends, resets, and starts again, they are on his bed making love. Throughout the entire time, Luther continues to croon. Neither of them realizes it at the time, but they don't just make love, they make a baby.

Five weeks have passed since *Luther Session*, which is how Asa thinks of the time she and Darryll spent in his room. The behavior was so *out-of-character* for her. In the past, she has avoided these kinds of entanglements like the plague, because she had no intention of finding herself in a predicament of this nature. Now she is torn between calling Darryll and seeking his advice, and just going ahead and making an appointment to get an abortion. But the latter is something that she cannot do lightly. She knows herself to have been an unwanted child, *but at least she didn't kill me*, she says to herself. *I wonder why I haven't heard anything from Darryll in almost three weeks. He did call me a couple of times since "Luther Session," but that was probably just to salve **his** conscious since he knows that I was a virgin when it happened*, she says to herself.

She calls Tamika, her best friend, and confides in her. Tamika advises her to get an abortion, but still, *she is torn*. "Maybe I'll wait awhile," she says. "I don't have to decide today. I just needed to talk with someone who cares."

In response Tamika tells her, "Girlfriend, I probably love you more than I do anyone else in the world, so don't you go ruining your life with a brat before you're twenty! If anybody from our neighborhood has a chance to make it, you do. *Get rid of it!* There's no way for you to get through the army and then through college with a crumb snatcher on your tail. It's not like you have a mom who's anxiously waiting for her first grandchild. So don't be stupid! I know you; I know how you think, but this is no time to be gallant!" *But still, Asa is averse to the idea.*

When the seventh week is approaching and she has heard no more from Darryll, she decides to call his home. His mother, Mamie Lee, answers the phone. "Whom did you say is calling?" she asks. Asa tells her that she is a friend of Darryll's, and that she is trying to get in contact with him. Mamie, never one to mince words responds with, "In my day, it was the young man who got in contact with the young woman, if he were interested." Asa doesn't know how to respond to this, but she is thinking: *the contact has already been made.* She doesn't say this however. What she says is, "Yes, ma'am, but this is really important. If I can have a number where I can reach him, I'd really appreciate it."

Mamie, however, has no intention of giving Darryll's phone number to any female who has not already received her personal stamp of approval. So she says, "I'm sorry, but I won't give you Darryll's phone number," and she hangs up before Asa has a chance to respond.

How can she be so rude? She doesn't even know me. She has no idea what the situation is, or how much of an emergency is involved. Asa is thinking these thoughts as she angrily redials the number. Mamie answers the phone with an annoyed, "Hello."

"Mrs. Crenshaw," Asa says without preamble, "I'm pregnant with Darryll's child. I'd hoped to discuss this with him before discussing it with anyone else, but since I can't reach him, perhaps you'll give him this message for me."

Mamie, who is by no means easily stunned, is momentarily stunned. She says, "If this is your idea of a joke, young woman, I don't think it's very funny!" Asa assures her that it is no joke, that she does not consider it a laughing matter either.

"I'm in the army, Ma'am, and I need to make a decision about what to do. I need to talk to him because it is his child that I'm carrying. That's why I asked you for his phone number," she divulges.

Mamie doesn't like this. But there is something in this young woman's voice that makes her know that this is no joke; that this is no lie. As a retired principal, she's had over thirty years of listening to young people's *truths* and *lies*, and she can spot a lie a mile away. Still, she is very protective when it comes to her family, her son in particular.

She says, "I'm sure you believe that what you've just told me is true; in fact, you may know it to be true, but there's no way that I can know it. So you understand my dilemma, I hope." Asa wants to tell her that the dilemma is not hers, but instead she says that she needs to talk to Darryll. Mamie tells her that she will ask Darryll to give her a call; Asa gives Mamie a phone number where she can be reached during the day.

Immediately Mamie calls Darryll, but he is out. She leaves a message that it is urgent; that he needs to call home at once. Later that day when he calls, she tells him about her conversation with Asa; she asks, "Is it true?" He tells her that it could be true, that he doesn't know for sure. But he lies. He knows that Asa had never slept with another man. He knows that he should have called her himself, and that he should have ascertained whether or not she had gotten pregnant. In fact, he had meant to do just that. But sleeping with a virtual stranger was so out-of-character for him.

He considers himself a responsible young man who does not involve himself in these kinds of situations. He was well aware of what the possible consequences might be. Besides, *he remembers the low-rent district where he picked Asa up for their date. He remembers her awe when he showed her around his parents' home. He does not think that he wants a long-term relationship with someone who has her background.* But he should have considered these things before he took her to bed. He is reluctant to call her because of the possible ramifications. Was *the yield* worth it?

Book II

The Yield

The Rest of the Story

The Yield
Book II
The Rest of the Story

Introduction

Chapter X 116

Sherl, Mary, and Frustration
Jan, John, and AIDS
Lynn and Missing Lucas

Chapter XI 129

Yen, Ron, and HIV
Robert, Jr., Robert, Sr., and the Gang
May, Gerald, and the Affair

Chapter XII 140

Dexter, Dawn, and Herpes
Carla, Roderick and Denial
Jewel, Steven and the Double Life

Chapter XIII 151

Sue and No-Commitment Phil
Amanda, Gloria, and Hubert-the-Trapped
Ruth, Josh, and Maybe Dexter

Chapter XIV 162

Ida and Disappearing Sydney
Wilber, Ester, and Daughter, Queen
Sheena, Boyd, and Liz

Book II - Yield

Teal

Chapter XV 171

Erica, Sam, and His Need for Freedom
Eunice and Eugene, the Weekend Alcoholic
Luther and Lacy. Perfection?

Chapter XVI 189

Matthew, Mable, and Discontent
Tisha, Tomas, and Yvonne
Nikki, Shree, and Mike

Chapter XVII 209

Stewart Stealing
Lauren, Luis, and Dr. Pat
Megan, Randy, and Gretel

Chapter XVIII 220

Donna, Neil, and Mannin
Gina, Alvin, and Infidelity
Renee, Earl, and Juanita
Asa and Darryll

To the Reader

Poem: The Yield

Introduction - Book II

Hundreds of Black couples divorce every day in this country. At this juncture it should be no secret why these relationships, unfortunately, do not last. Marriage is built on trust. When the trust is gone, the marriage, in its truest sense, has ended. Yet, when these relationships evaporate, the children resulting from them are still very much facts of life. All too frequently, these children are hardly, if at all, considered when the decision is made to fragment their families.

It is an undisputable fact that it takes two people to create a life. Two people are needed to nourish that life to its maturity. The decision to fragment a child's family ought not be made with him or her being given little or no consideration. This decision is life-altering, frequently life shattering, for most children, and many of them are never again the happy, carefree children that every child has a right to be!

In my multiple and varied experiences as a classroom teacher, I have heard numerous parents say of their difficult and hostile children, "I don't know what's wrong with him," or, "I have not idea what's wrong with her." These parents have not even considered the fact that for a considerable number of months, and sometimes *for several years* as well, *a child's family is his or her whole world*. And this world has been shattered by their divorce. Some parents are capable, it seems, of having self-inflicted, selective amnesia. This being the case, they can select to forget about their vows, about all of the attention they lavished upon their child for months or years, about the child's love for both *Mom* and *Dad*. But the child has no such mechanism in place to ride him or her over the rough terrain. The child remembers clearly being tossed into the air by a beloved dad, being ridden on the back and shoulders of a beloved dad, being played with in the park, being allowed to *drive* the car, being kissed and hugged good night, being rocked to sleep cradled in the arms of a beloved dad! *The child remembers,* even when he or she is incapable of articulating the memory. And now, *of course* there's something wrong with the child! He's being impacted by the collaspe of his world! Who among us wouldn't be?

Usually when a couple breaks up, distrust has become a factor within the relationship, but distrust isn't something that just happens. There are reasons why distrust becomes a component. The Black man's family has a need to believe in his integrity, a need to feel that what they think of him *is important to him!* His family has a need as well as a desire to trust him, and to feel that he is worthy of their trust. He needs to be cognizant of the fact that *he is the only one who can assure his family that they have his love, loyalty, and support,* that there is no reason why they cannot trust him. When he behaves as if this is not so, the family structure is weakened. When the head of the family fails to lead in a way which his sons and daughters can emulate and in a way which his wife can respect, future generations are threatened. This is so because children *learn* what they *live,* and they *live* what they are *allowed to experience.*

The constant lying, the constant game-playing, the constant need to evade, the constant cheating which is normal behavior for far too many Black men, are behaviors which many of them observed in their fathers, uncles, and other dominant male role models in their lives. *This destructive cycle* can be broken *only by the Black man.* If his sons are to be free of the psychological garbage which accumulates in a climate where these behaviors are observed and accepted as normal, masculine behaviors, then the choice is a foregone conclusion: the Black man must choose not to engage in these behaviors. This is not an option if the Black race, the Black family, is to survive!

You see, the Black family's survival is threatened when Black men father children for whom they feel no responsibility, nor assume any. It is threatened when children are born to women to whom these children's fathers feel no allegiance. It is threatened when the birth of a child does not assist to cement an already solid, marital relationship. It is threatened when Black boys enter manhood with misplaced or warped ideas of what it means to be a man! The Black family is threatened when children are being born, but their births are no longer considered, "A family affair." If the Black race, the Black family is to survive, the refrain must not be, *That's just my baby's daddy.* It must be instead, *This is my beloved husband, the father of our beloved child!*

Chapter X

Sherl, Mary, and Frustration

"Exactly what time did I tell you to be home, Young Lady?" Sherl screams, as Mary exits the car. Mary makes no response as she flounces past Sherl and heads for her room. "You wait just one minute!" Sherl says. "I asked you a question!"

Mary waits sullenly, one foot on the bottom stair, her back to her mother. She says nothing. Again Sherl prods: "What time did I say for you to be home?" Mary Shrugs.

"Look at me; answer me!" Sherl yells.

"You don't have to yell," Mary says. "I can hear you."

"Then act like it! I've asked you more than once. What are you waiting for?" Sherl asks.

Book II - Yield

Teal

Mary begins to cry. Through her tears, sniffling intermittently, she says, "I want Dad. I can always talk to Dad. Is he asleep?"

"Your father isn't home yet," Sherl tells her.

"Then why are you yelling at me? At least I beat him home," Mary responds.

"Mary," Sherls says, "talk to me. You never acted like this before. Tell me what's bothering you. You know I love you; I only want to help. What's the matter?"

Crying harder now, Mary says, "Mom, I'm pregnant; I've already seen a doctor. Oh Mom, what am I going to do?"

Sherl goes to Mary and puts her arm around her. She is now crying herself. Through her tears she says, "I'm here for you, Baby. Together we'll work this out; you go on to bed now. We'll talk more in the morning."

As Mary starts up the stairs, Sherl says, "Mary?" Mary turns at the sound of her name. Sherl continues, "I love you; we will work this out. *Together*. You go to sleep now, you hear."

It is close to 3 a.m. when Rufus arrives home. Both Mary and Sherl have fallen asleep, but Sherl has slept fitfully and is awakened by the sound of the front door closing, though Rufus does his best to close it silently. She raises up and looks at the clock. As Rufus enters the bedroom, Sherl says sleepily, "What on earth could you possibly have been doing this time of the morning?" Rufus does not respond, but goes into the bathroom and shuts the door, *hoping that Sherl will have fallen asleep again by the time he comes out.* And she has. She is exhausted.

It is late, close to 11 a.m. by the time the entire household is awake the following morning, a Saturday. Both of the younger children have soccer games later that day. They chatter together excitedly about their upcoming games. Mary has been awake for more than an hour but has not come out of her room. Sherl says to Rufus, "Why were you so late coming in? Where were you?" Rufus tells her that he was just hanging out with the guys, playing pinochle. *But he is lying.* He was in Atlantic City, gambling. Rufus has gambled away the mortgage payment, which Sherl thinks has already been paid for the month.

Sherl says, "Rufus, I need to talk with you about Mary. She is troubled; she's experiencing some problems right now." But Rufus is in no mood to talk about their daughter's problems. *He has problems of his own.* He needs to concentrate on recouping that mortgage money before Sherl learns that he has not already made the payment. Half-heartedly, he asks what the matter is. Sherl relates all of her suspicions to him. She tells him about Mary arriving home a two in the morning. She tells him of the sullenness, which is new in Mary. She concludes with Mary's statement: *Then why are you yelling at me? It's Dad you should be yelling at. At least I beat him home.*

In response to this Rufus says, "Are you telling me that Mary thinks she should be able to stay out as late as I can?"

"Rufus," Sherl says, "you have missed the point entirely. What I am hoping you'll understand is that Mary is aware of the late hours you're keeping. She is *very definitely conscious of your absence in her life.* I think a lot of her misbehavior is an effort to fill that void."

Book II - Yield

On one level, Rufus does understand this. He loves Mary. He is always proud when one of their friends refers to Mary as a *Daddy's girl*. But he has gotten more heavily involved in gambling than he intended. He had meant only to have a little fun, to unwind a little. But he has acquired the habit now; he is hooked. *He spends most of his free time, and a good deal of the time when he's at work, trying to figure out ways of juggling their finances to cover his losses, losses which, up to this point, Sherl is unaware of.*

"Has Mary been examined yet? Has she told you who the boy is or how old he is. Does the boy's parents know? I didn't think Mary would even be thinking about sex yet, and certainly not involved in it. Is she sure she's pregnant?" he asks.

"Apparently so," Sherl says. "She told me she's already seen a doctor. You go talk to Mary. Last night she asked for you; said she could always talk to you," Sherl concludes.

But Rufus is reluctant. He knows that involvement means being at home to see what develops and to help control what develops, and he doesn't want that. *I can't afford that,* he says to himself. He needs to be elsewhere if he is to stand a chance of recouping his losses, so he says, "You handle it. Whatever the two of you decide will probably be for the best."

Rufus is already *thinking about who might lend him money with which to gamble later that day.* Sherl has to handle Mary's problem as best she can. Rufus' interest are elsewhere. He says he loves his family, but they are secondary to his pursuit of *the yield.*

Book II - Yield

Teal

Jan, John, and AIDS

On Friday around 6 p.m., John arrives home from his business trip. Jan has dropped the kids off at her mother's and has arranged for them to spend the night there. As soon as John comes through the door, before he has a chance to set his suitcase down Jan says, "John, I've tested positive for the AIDS virus. I've never been unfaithful to you. How did I get it?"

All of the blood drains from John's face. All week he has felt vaguely ill, but he figured he was coming down with a cold. His symptons have been much like the ones he experiences when that is the case. Now he begins to feel fearful. Momentarily he is speechless, then he says, "Oh God, Jan. Oh God." This second *Oh God,* is more like a whispered moan.

He goes to Jan and attempts to take her in his arms. She backs away saying, "Do you realize what you've done? Don't you know that our two, beautiful babies will very likely be orphans in a couple of years, *tops*?"

The following Monday, John does not go to work. He goes to Dr. Potts for an AIDS test. Mary accompaines him. As they drive to and from the Doctor's office, neither of them utters a word, but the silence is not comfortable as their past ones have been.

Days pass, days in which Jan and John are silent strangers in their own home, separated only by feet, but miles apart. The children, Evette and Evelyn, *wonder why Mama and Daddy no longer laugh and talk to one another.* They wonder *why Mama looks so sad all the time now and why Daddy looks so angry.* They are sad because *Mama* is sad. They are quiet and subdued because *Daddy* is mad and they don't know what they've done to cause the anger or how to make it go away.

Book II - Yield

Teal

When John's test results reveal that he, too, *is HIV positive*, both he and Jan begin treatment. They have agreed to keep their disease secret as long as they can. John's insurance will not pay for catastrophic illnesses until an employee has been with the company for at least eighteen months. John has been with the company for only fourteen months. Both think about *how pleased each of them was when he landed the job, and how bright the future seemed at that time. Now, all they can think about is how dismal the future looms.* They have decided, for the sake of their girls, to stay together, but there is no joy in the union. Both are heavy-hearted people whose relationship has succumbed to the corrosiveness *the yield* is capable of producing.

Lynn and Missing Lucas

As Anne and Todd spend increasingly more time together, Anne begins, for the first time, to play hooky from school. Lynn learns of it when she gets this message from Anne's school: *Mrs. Krupp, your daughter, Anne, is not at school today. If she is ill or has another legitimate reason for the absence, please contact the school by phone, or send a note when she returns so that she can be given credit for an excused absence.*

Lynn replays the tape, listening to the message again to be sure that it is meant for her, that it is about her child, her Anne. *This is probably some other Anne*, she is thinking. *They probably called the wrong parent. There must be ten or fifteen Annes at that school. My Anne was certainly at school today. I dropped her off myself.* All of this goes through Lynn's mind as she flips through her address book looking for the number to the school. When the connection is made, she is asked to hold, then she is connected with the attendance secretary.

Lynn begins, "This is Lynn Krupp, Anne Krupp's mother. I received a message that Anne is not at school today. I know it's a mistake because I dropped my daughter off at school this morning myself.

"If you can hold for a while longer, Mrs. Krupp, I can verify Anne's attendance today, or her absence," the attendance secretary says. "I'll get to-day's absentee list and doublecheck it." About two minutes later the secretary says, "Anne Krupp is on this list. We have only one Anne Krupp at this school, but I'll be glad to check with her advisory teacher to ask if Anne was tardy today. Sometimes when a child is tardy, he or she is marked absent and placed on the absentee list, and it isn't changed until later during the day."

"But Anne shouldn't have been tardy today. I dropped her off plenty early enough," Lynn says.

Lynn is waiting for her as Anne arrives home at the usual time later that day. She meets Anne at the front door. She has already decided that a direct confrontation is best. "Anne," she says, "Why were you not at school today?" Anne feels and looks as if she has been caught red-handed. She has no idea how her mother knows that she didn't attend classes today, but she can see that it's pointless to lie; *she lies anyhow.* She says that she and a few friends went to the mall.

"Anne, the mall is not open at seven-thirty; that's when I dropped you off. Now, I'm going to ask you this only once more: Where were you today?"

Again Anne realizes the futility of lying. "I spent the day with Todd, Mom. He picked me up after you dropped me off," she admits. Lynn had not even suspected this. *This is not normal behavior for Anne.* Anne has always been an honor student. She has always enjoyed school. Lynn is completely baffled.

"Anne," she says, I'm going to call your father right now! We're going to get to the bottom of this. We will not tolerate this kind of behavior from you; you are too important to us to be allowed to behave in this manner. Besides, you have a younger brother and sister who will want to emulate your behavior. Is this what you want to see them do?"

Anne hangs her head, refusing to look at her mother. She's always been proud of the fact that she knew she was setting a good example for her younger siblings. Now she feels terrible. Her mother has frequently complimented her for the fine example she was setting for the younger children, so she knows how disappointed in her *her* mother is.

Lynn dials Lucas' job and is told that he called in sick. For the second time today, Lynn is completely baffled. Lucas had left home that morning heading to work, *as far as Lynn knew*. She begins to *wonder if he had an accident or if something else has happened which might have caused him to have to call in sick after leaving home.*

But Lucas is not sick. He has taken off to spend the day with Beth. The two of them planned this day weeks ago. At this very moment, they are in bed together. They have made love, and are intending to sleep until noon. But Lynn, of course, has no knowledge of this. She knows only that she needs him, their daughter needs him, and he is unavailable to them.

As Lynn hangs the phone up she says to Anne, "Go to your room; we'll continue this conversation later."

In her bedroom, Anne lies across the bed sobbing. *I've made such a mess of things,* she says to herself. *I wish I had just kept my promise.* She had promised her mother after the abortion that she would never be intimate with a man again to whom she wasn't married. She had meant it at the time, but she had *had* no idea how difficult that promise would be to keep. She hears the hallway phone ringing and wonders if Todd is calling, but she dare not ask. It is indeed Todd. Lynn recognizes his voice and says, "Todd, let me speak with your mother." *She is in no mood to be cordial with Todd.*

Todd has not expected to speak with Anne's mother. Anne always answers the phone when it rings if she is at home, and most of the time the call is for her. "Mrs. Krupp, my mother isn't home yet," he says in nervously. "Can I take a message?" he asks politely.

"Yes. Tell her for me that you drove Anne away from the school today without permission, and that I *don't* appreciate that. Let her know that she can expect a call from me later this evening. You probably didn't have her permission to leave school today yourself. Goodbye."

Todd is totally troubled. He had no idea that Lynn knew about this situation. In fact, the purpose of his call had been to ascertain if everything was okay with Lynn. *What am I going to tell Ma?* he asks himself.

Later that day Lucas arrives home at the usual time. Lynn waits about half an hour before asking him about his day. She is hoping that he will volunteer this information. When he doesn't broach the subject she says,

"How was work today, Lucas?" When he says that it was *just the usual*, she asks what that means.

Lucas does not want to discuss his day. He *knows* Lynn, so he knows that she is suspicious of something, or she would not be questioning a response like *the usual*. Instead of responding to her question, he asks, "What's for dinner?"

Instead of responding to his question, Lynn says, "I asked you a question. What is *the usual* for you at work these days?" When he begins to list some of the things he normally does at work, she interrupts with, "Cut it, Lucas. You didn't go to work today. Where *did* you go?"

Lucas had no idea that Lynn was aware of his absence from work today. Usually when he does not go to work, he instructs his secretary that if anyone calls for him she is to say, *Mr. Krupp is out of the building at this time, or Mr. Krupp is away from his desk right now*. But this time he'd forgotten to remind her, as he has always done in the past, because he had planned this absence weeks ago. "What are you talking about?" he asks, stalling for time, trying to think of a plausible excuse in case she refuses to drop it and insists on one. Lynn says nothing but stares at him. He is the first to look away.

The silence is agonizing to Lucas. Finally he says, "I had some things to take care of, so I went in late. Lynn continues to stare at him, saying nothing. When the silence again becomes deafening he asks, "What's bothering you, Lynn? Why all the questions? Is there a problem that I'm unaware of?"

In response Lynn says, "What things, Lucas? What things can you take care of at seven o'clock in the morning? That's the time you left here!" Not giving him a chance to answer, she then goes on to say, "There's a lot bothering me, and part of what's bothering me is my husband leaving home with the pretense of heading to work, but not being at work when I called the office for him. What things do you need to take care of that you can't tell me about?"

Lucas continues to lie: "You're making a mountain out of a molehill. What do you want me to say? What do you want from me? I go to work everyday; I bring my money home, I take care of you and the children. What more do you want from me?"

I want loyalty; I want truthfulness; I want fidelity, is her fleeting thought, but she doesn't speak her thoughts. She doesn't know what, but her woman's intuition tells her that something is amiss. She tries once again. "Lucas," she says, "I don't need any problems from you. Our daughter is all the problem I can handle just now."

At this point she relates what has transpired concerning Anne. She concludes with, "So she needs more of you. She needs you to be totally involved in her life; she needs to know that you care, that you are there for her. She needs you to be at home more, we all do. We hardly see you at all on weekends anymore. All of this stuff started with Anne since you've been too busy elsewhere to spend any quality time with her, with any of us really.

If there is someone else with whom you want to spend your leisure time, tell me now."

But Lucas does not tell her. Lying has become a way of life for him. He loves Anne in his own peculiar way. He would like to be there for her. He knows that the philandering must be relinquished in order for him to be at home the way he used to be prior to getting involved with Beth. At this juncture, he's made promises to Beth, *other lies* that he has no intentions of keeping, but he doesn't feel that he can just drop her. Beth works for the same company he does, in the same office; she could cause problems on the job if he does that. Besides, he knows that Beth is not a mild-mannered woman. She's not going to stand for him to just drop her and go on as if she doesn't exist. He feels that he's caught between a rock and a hard place. *And he is,* but he intentionally maneuvered himself into that position. Lucas wants his family, he wants to he there for his daughter, but he wants the life of a single gigolo too. The allure of *the yield* is the catalyst which propels him to neglect his family.

# Chapter XI

Yen, Ron, and HIV

Ron and Yen are both *HIV positive*. They are expecting their baby to be born in about two weeks. Since learning this distressing news, Yen has slept and eaten poorly. She and Ron, who had been so happy when they first learned of the expected baby, are now like silent, hostile strangers who are forced to live in close proximity. They rarely speak to one another, usually only if it is absolutely necessary.

Yen, like so many other women, and some men too, think that being married, being a partner in a committed relationship, means that they are protected. *And it should!* But it doesn't! You see, there are different levels of commitment, and people in relationships need to communicate with one another, and to articulate clearly what commitment means to each of them. Yen may have indeed been committed to the relationship to the extent that she would never have allowed herself to become intimate with anyone other than Ron. This is so because to Yen commitment means loyalty, trust; exclusivity. On the other hand, Ron may have been committed to the extent that he was willing to say *I do* and to let the world know that Yen is his woman (*but not necessarily his only woman*).

Allow me to explain further. Perhaps in Ron's mind, this level of commitment is all he needs; *all he understands*. And the operative word here is *he*. *He* obviously did not consider Yen's needs: the need to be, if nothing else, protected from a life-threatening disease which is sexually transmitted; the need to have her unborn child protected from all potential harm from which she or Ron could possibly protect him or her.

Today Yen feels driven to ask, "Ron, didn't you realize that cheating, sleeping around in the nineties could be lethal? Did we mean so little to you that you were willing to risk our health, and yours, for the sake of a piece of tail?" Ron is silent for so long that Yen has begun to think that he isn't going to respond. Finally he answers her.

"Yes, I knew," he says reluctantly, (he doesn't like talking about it), "but it happened only once, I swear, and I guess I didn't really think it would happen to me. I just didn't think! *God, I'm sorry.* I'd do anything if I could undo this. Won't you give me a chance to make it up to you?"

"Ron, I don't think either of us is going to have a chance to *make it up* to anybody, especially to our child who is innocent in all of this, but probably the most damaged. Chances are good that our child won't live long enough to know either of us, or we won't live long enough to get to raise our child. You're talking as if you don't understand that what we have is incurable. Oh!" Yen screams, *doubling over*.

"What is it? Do you think the baby's coming?" Ron asks. Yen says nothing, but shakes her head to indicate that *she thinks so*. Ron grabs her already packed suitcase, runs out and puts it in the car, then returns to assist Yen. He drives her to the hospital, concern for her and the baby evident on his troubled countenance. As drives, he phones the hospital to alert them that Yen is in labor and that they are on their way to the hospital.

As he awaits the birth of their baby, he sits, head in hands, praying that somehow the baby will escape the terrible fate which could await him or her. *But it is not to be.*

Following twelve hours of hard labor, Yen gives birth to a four pound baby girl. The infant is weak, and ill, and has to be sustained in an incubator. The baby, whom they have named Teresa, has tested positive for the HIV virus. She lives for only five days.

As the tiny casket is being lowered into the ground, Yen is inconsolable. Ron too is devastated. He had no idea he'd feel as he does about the baby. He had no idea she'd be so tiny and helpless and beautiful, and look at him as if she already knew he was to be her protector from the world. He can't stand knowing that he is the reason for her life-ending disease. Never before has he wanted anything as intensely as he wanted Teresa to survive and be healthy. He knows that all this pain, all this devastation, could have probably been avoided. He knows that Baby Teresa, Yen, and he as well, are all victims of the ravages of *the yield.*

Robert, Jr., Robert, Sr., and the Gang

When Bobby's mother cannot reach Robert Sr. at work, she begins to weep quietly. As she is searching through her purse for a tissue, the desk sergeant hands one to her and says, "Ma'am, we're going to have to talk with him alone. I'll be back shortly, just sit over there." As he says this, he points to some folding chairs that have seen their best days and have been placed along a a faded, yellow wall.

As June sits waiting for the sergeant's return, she *wonders where Robert is.* As far as she knew, he was supposed to be at work. But he did not go to work. He and Shana, his new lady love, have both called in sick. Both use cocaine recreationally. Shana introduced Robert to it. She has used it recreationally for years now, and has always been able to take it or leave it, *so far.* But Robert is needing more and more of it, increasingly. He can't wait, each time, for it to take effect. At first he used it on weekends only, and on an occasional day off. But *now he uses it whenever he can get it.*

As June sits waiting, she *thinks about the pending divorce. She wonders why things went wrong. She wonders where she went wrong.* She has no idea that she didn't go wrong. Robert just wants a different woman. He is bored with the monotony of marriage and family. He wants a different woman in his bed. She *thinks about how much fun they once had, how much joy they once shared. She thinks about the mutual pleasure the birth of their son brought them.* She *thinks about how, increasingly, Bobby has been troubled and troubling since his dad left their home.* Her reveries are interrupted by the sergeant's return.

Book II - Yield

Teal

"It has been decided that Bobby will be released in your custody, Ma'am, but any future brushes with the law, and I doubt he'll fare as well," the sergeant warns her.

Hours later, Bobby attempts to reach his dad at his apartment, but gets only the answering machine. He slams the phone down without leaving a message and says to his mom, "Dad is never at home. He promised we'd see each other as much as ever, but I never see him, and I don't care either!"

June tries to console him, but he rejects her and streaks past her into his room. She feels terrible, as if it is she who has done him an injustice. *She yearns to be able to comfort him like she did when he was little. She wishes for the time when a kiss made it better, for a time when she knew his dad could, and would, go into his room, and no matter how upset Robert, Jr. was, make him smile.* It makes her feel so sad to know that there is nothing she can do to comfort him now, and that his dad is no longer around to offer him the comfort which has always been available to him. It increases her heavyheartedness to realize that the one person he probably needs most has, of his own volition, removed himself removed himself from their son's immediate environment. She knows that he should be reprimanded for what he did, and in *the old days,* he would've never gotten away so lightly, but she feels apologetic, that all of this is a by-product of their failed relationship, that her son is somehow the victimized in all of this.

It is not until the following day, after six o'clock in the evening, that Bobby reaches his dad at home. "Ask your mom to drive you over here. Bring a pair of pajamas and a change of clothes, and plan to spend the night with me, he says, fleetingly feeling conscience-stricken.

Book II - Yield

Teal

When Bobby arrives, his dad has already ordered Chinese food, take-out. Several small, white cartons are on the coffee table. Bobby is disappointed. He was hoping that his dad would take him to Mickey D's. He loves the Big Macs and fries there, they're his favorites. But he says, "Yes," when his dad asks if he feels like Chinese tonight.

As they eat, Bobby notices that his dad hardly takes more than a couple of bites. They used to race to see who would get the most; now he *wonders why his dad is eating so little.* Bobby has no way of knowing that his dad had a hit of cocaine shortly before he arrived, and that food is the last thing on his mind. Robert, Sr. had really intended to restrain himself, not to take a hit tonight. He doesn't want to be under the influence of the drug with Bobby around, but he is hooked now. He no longer has the control to take it or leave it. It controls him now, but he isn't yet aware that this is so.

Bobby watches his dad with his peripheral vision; *he wonders why his eyes are so bright, why it seems that he can't sit still for more than a couple of minutes.* Bobby feels a little frightened of his dad for the first time in his life. He used to love spending time alone with his dad. His dad often said, "We love Mom, but we men need to get together often for our man to man talks, don't we?"

Bobby *wishes things were as they used to be when he and his mom and dad had great times together. He doesn't understand why things had to change; he doesn't know what he did wrong, but he thinks he must've done something to make his dad leave their home. He doesn't understand why things can't go back to the way they used to be. He doesn't understand why he feels so angry so often now. He wonders if he and his dad could have one of their man- to- man talks, and if he could explain all of this to his dad, and if he apologizes for whatever it was that he did, will his dad come back home then.*

Robert has started using money which he and June have set aside for Bobby's college education, to support his blossoming cocaine habit. His job performance is suffering. For the first time since beginning his job, more than ten years ago, he does not receive a performance bonus when they are handed out at the company's annual banquet. For the first time since beginning the job, he and June do not attend the banquet together.

When he takes his son home on the following day, June invites him to come into the house. "We need to talk about our son. Can you stay for a while?" she wants to know.

Bobby has gone into his room; he comes out bouncing a basketball. "I'm going to the park, Mom," he says, continuing to bounce the ball. June tells him to stop bouncing the ball in the house; she admonishes him not to go any place else but to the park near their house. She tells him to come home before it gets dark.

After Bobby leaves, June tells his dad about the shoplifting incident; she tells him about the episodes of trouble at school. She asks why he is seeing so little of his son. Defensively he says, "So you're saying that I'm to blame for all of his problems".

"Robert," she says, "I have no interest in assigning blame. My interest is strictly our son. I'm interested in seeing him regain his well-behaved friends and his good grades. I want Bobby free of the anger with which he seems to be filled now." Wringing her hands, her voice quivering with emotion, she appeals to him for help. But Robert is no longer capable of giving her the assistance which she is seeking. He is no longer capable even of helping himself. He is sinking deeper and deeper into the cocaine abyss. He and his family are suffering the demolition *the yield* is capable of inflicting.

Book II - Yield

Teal

May, Gerald, and the Affair

May and Gerald's divorce became final two weeks ago. They have joint custody of the twins, *but Gerald rarely sees them*. He promises himself faithfully that he is going to pick them up and spend his scheduled time with them, but invaribly, something comes up and he has to cancel at the last minute.

The twins have a birthday coming up soon. They will be five years old. May is thinking about this as she puts them to bed. She has a new man in her life and is trying to decide if she should allow him to meet Lara and Sara. He already knows about them and has asked to meet them, but she does not want them to meet every casual date that she has. She refuses to bring a string of *uncles* into their lives. She tells herself that she will introduce them to him when the time is right, *if it ever is*.

This time Gerald has managed to pick the twins up for his scheduled visit with them and because May has the weekend free of parental responsibilities, she has agreed that Carter can come to her home to pick her up for their date: *dinner and a movie*. After the movie, Carter asks if he can come in for a nightcap when they are approaching her house, but May tells him, "Not tonight; some other time though."

As Carter backs out of the driveway, Gerald pulls into the driveway with the twins. "Who was that?" Gerald asks.

"Who was who?" May asks in response, though she knows exactly of whom Gerald is inquiring.

"That man who just pulled out of *my* driveway," Gerald says.

May ignores the comment and asks, "Is something wrong? The kids aren't due back until tomorrow evening. Why are you here with them?" By this time the twins have gone into the kitchen where May keeps a box of their toys under the table, have taken out several toys, and are sitting on the floor playing with them. Lara is rubbing her left ear with one hand and is clutching a favored toy with another.

Gerald tells her that Lara, who has a history of earaches since the early months of life, has one now and has been crying for the past hour. "She stopped only when I told her we were coming home so I could put some drops in her ear. Do you still have some of those drops we used to put in her ears?" he asks.

May tells him that she does have some, that she *knows* that it is prudent to keep some on hand for times such as this one. She also tells him, "You should do the same if you're intending to share their care with me. I don't expect you to run here every time one of them has a little problem."

At this Gerald bristles; he gets defensive. "Tonight is the only time I've ever done this. What do you mean, *every time one of them has a problem?*" he asks.

May does not respond, she does not say what she is thinking: *that this is probably the first time that Beth has had an earache when he had the singlehanded responsibility for her care.* Instead, she goes into the bathroom to get the drops from the medicine cabinet where they are stored.

Returning to the kitchen she says, "Gerald, you might as well leave the girls here now that they are here." Gerald had meant to do just that. But he hadn't known how to approach the subject without making it appear that he was anxious to get rid of them. He really does love them, but they're a handful, and he had thought that he could save himself the drive back over the following day, if May were amenable to the girls being left at this time. Besides, he'd never had to be responsible, all by himself, for caring for the two of them simultaneously when he and May had been married. There was always May, or his mother, or her mother, on an aunt, or one of May's teen nieces dropping by, always someone to share their care.

"Fine, if that's what you want," he says nonchalantly, as if the idea had not occurred to him. He wants to ask May again about the man in the car who was backing out of the driveway, *his* driveway, when he and the girls were returning earlier tonight, but he doesn't want to antagonize her while she is being so agreeable. But he is thinking: *I'm not having any niggers here over my girls. I want May to get that straight. I won't say anything else tonight, but I'll make sure she gets that straight!"*

Gerald, however, is not overly concerned that May will have someone over who might put the twins at risk, in any manner. He knows how much she loves them, how protective she is of them. His concern is that May herself, will get close to another man; another man will get close to May. Even though he is involved with other women, and was involved with them while he and May were married, he still feels proprietary where May and the girls are concerned. He feels that they are *his*. Mentally, he has all but discounted the fact that *he no longer has any say so, whatsoever, about who can and cannot visit the home which was once his. It no longer is.* He liked being a family man, part of a family network. He would like to have his family back, yet his grip on *the yield* is as firm as it ever was.

Chapter XII

Dawn, Dexter, and Herpes

When Dexter arrives home later that day, he calls out, "Baby, I'm home!" This, which is usually met with the sounds of Dawn's feet rushing to greet him with a hug and a kiss, is met with silence. *That's strange*, Dexter says to himself; *she didn't say anything about not being home this evening.* This was indeed strange because Dawn always made a special effort to be at home when Dexter got home from work every day. But Dawn has *moved out.* She has packed all of her clothes and has left the city. Dexter doesn't discover this until several hours later when he goes to the closet to get his coat. The evening has turned chilly, and he knows it will be colder still by the time he returns home. Hunger is driving him now, even though he is still concerned about why Dawn isn't home and hasn't called.

Book II - Yield

Teal

As Dexter realizes that Dawn's clothes are missing, he runs to the closet in the guest bedroom to see if the clothes she hangs there are gone also; *they are*. This time it is he who is incredulous. *What have I done? he asks himself. Why would she do this? I love her so much; I know she loves me too. What has happened?* he wonders. He has forgotten, completely, about the hunger pangs. All he can think of now is *Dawn, where she is, what she is thinking, what would cause her to do this?* He calls her best friend's home, but Meg's answering machine picks up. He slams the phone down in frustration.

For the first time since their marriage, Dexter goes to bed in their home, alone. Lying there, he feels desolate, forlorn; betrayed. Never, in his wildest imaginations, did it ever occur to him that Dawn would abandon him, leave him without so much as a wave, a handshake. He felt certain of the depth of her commitment to the relationship and to him. Now, all he can do is wonder; agonize.

For several days now, Dexter has felt unwell, but he attributes it to the fact that his wife has left him and he has no idea where she is. He thinks of making an appointment to see the doctor, but he has a physical, his annual one, scheduled for the following Monday, three days away.

As a result of his physical examination, Dexter learns that he has herpes, genital herpes. He immediately begins to think about the indiscretions, the one-night stands he allowed himself to become involved in before and during his marriage. He tells himself *it's been just a few since he and Dawn married, and most of the time he was careful to use a condom.*

Dexter, like some other brothers, behave as if their philosophy is: *I am immune. It can happen to others, but not me.* They live their lives as though they believe they are safe if they are careful and behave responsibly *most of the time*. Their thinking is much like that of an immature child who covers his head and says, "You can't see me now," though the rest of the body is still in full view. Their thinking is: *what she doesn't know can't hurt her*. Well, *she does know, and she is hurting!*

Dawn's incredulousness turned to horrification when she received the results of the culture from her doctor. *How can this be?* she initially wonders. Not once did she think of her husband as the source of her infection. She loves him with all her heart. She believed that he felt the same way. She, naively, *was hoping that he had not been infected*. Never once did it occur to her that he was the *source of her infection*. She feels insulted as well as violated!

Now she packs her clothes, crying hysterically and throwing things into bags without even bothering to fold them. Most of her friends call her a *neat freak* because she always does things so neatly, but not this time. All she could think of was *getting out, and far away, before Dexter got home. I can't bear to look at him now. If he could do this, he's got to be a monster. If he can chance exposing himself, and me consequently, to whatever it is that someone else has, just so he can get what is available to him at home, away from home, then he's got to be a monster, or a seriously disturbed man, and in either case, my best bet is to leave here,* she says to herself.

As Dexter realizes the ramifications of what he has learned, he is no longer clueless. He has more than an intimation of why she is gone. He comprehends that their relationship has been destroyed by *the yield*.

Book II - Yield

Teal

Carla, Roderick, and Denial

Carla continues to urge Roderick to go to counseling with her. Carrie, now fifteen, is being impacted by the tension in their home. She is changing from the bubbly, loquacious, curious child that she has always been, becoming more introverted, staying in her room more, interacting with others less, even Carla and Roderick.

It is now summer, and today is the beginning of their annual, two-week vacation period. They have recently bought a new car and are planning to take Carrie to Disney World in Florida. Normally, Carrie would have been too excited to sleep; she'd be up at the crack of dawn awakening them with, "Let's get this show on the road," or some such expression.

When Carla gets up, she heads for the bathroom. On her way there, she has to go past Carrie's bedroom; she peeks in. Carrie is still in bed. She is wide awake, staring at the ceiling, lying flat of her back with open palms clasped underneath her head. When Carla opens the door, Carrie closes her eyes, feigning sleep, but not quickly enough. *Carla realizes that she is awake, but closes the door gently, as if not to awaken her.*

When she returns to their bedroom, Roderick is sitting up in bed. "Why're you up so early?" he asks. "What time do you guys think we should leave?" he asks.

"It isn't that early, Carla says. "It's almost nine o'clock. I'm thinking we should leave in a couple of hours, no later than noon. I peeked into Carrie's room on my way to the bathroom a few minutes ago. She pretended to be asleep, but she wasn't. I saw her eyes close as I opened her door. I think Carrie is troubled about something. Have you noticed anything different about her lately?" Carla asks.

"Probably just normal teenage behavior," he says in response. "You know how kids are these days. You should hear some of the stories women tell me at work about their kids, then you'd know that Carrie's just acting the way teenagers act," he tells her.

"Some of it maybe," Carla says, "but not all of it. I've been noticing her more and more lately, and I don't like the changes I see."

"Don't create problems where none exists," Roderick says. To this, Carrie does not respond, *but she is sure that something is not right with Carrie.* She knows her daughter, and she knows her well. The two of them are close, *very close*, and she knows when something isn't right with her.

Roderick has noticed some of the same changes which Carla has observed, but Roderick is quick to deny anything that doesn't fit into the nice little psychological pegholes he needs to have filled. He can pretend, to the extent of fooling himself even that everything is okay. This is Roderick's way of handling personal problems: *to deny their existence!*

Like the problems which exist between Roderick and her, Carla realizes that she must do whatever she can to solve the problems which Carrie is experiencing. She recognizes that she cannot count on Roderick for assistance when it comes to solving family problems. She is cognizant that *her* Roderick cannot deal effectively with conflicts of a personal nature. He is good at helping outsiders solve their problems, but when the problems are up close and personal, for him denial is *the yield*.

Book II - Yield

Teal

Jewel, Steven, and the Double Life

Jewel's parents are encouraging her to get out more, but she has no interest in dating. Even though much of her depression following the miscarriage has lifted, she doesn't feel ready to interact with anyone other than family. "Why don't you go to the community college this fall?" her mother suggests. "Classes will be starting in about five weeks, so you probably will have just enough time to get registered, if you go over and do it in person."

Jewel's heart isn't in it, but to please her mother she registers for three classes. As the week for freshmen orientation approaches, she can feel herself getting excited. *I haven't felt this excited about anything in a long time,* she says to herself, as she and her mom leave the mall. They have been shopping for jeans and sweatshirts. They have found a nice selection of each, and one of the sweatshirts has the name of the college and its mascot emblazoned across the back in neon colors.

The week of orientation is filled with new experiences for Jewel. She realizes *she's enjoying the whirlwind of activities.* She has met several other entering freshmen who are also over twenty, and she does not feel at all out of place, as she feared she would.

Classes are another pleasant surprise for Jewel. While she was not a good student in high school, she is doing very well in the three classes she's taking, and is even enjoying doing the homework assignments, something she hated doing, and frequently did not do, in high school. At the end of the first semester, which ended a couple of weeks before Christmas, Jewel has a B+ GPA, and has been told by her advisor that she will be allowed to register for three additional hours of college credit, if she chooses to do so. Jewel is delighted by this news. Her parents are really happy too, and for the first time since Jewel's and Steven's breakup, *they feel hopeful.*

Jewel can't believe how well she's doing in her classes. She *can't believe how right it feels to be a part of the college scene.* She has lived in a college town all of her life nearly, and never once thought she might enjoy going to college, being involved in college life. Now she wonders *why she never even considered it before.* More than once she has thanked her mother for the suggestion that she register for a few classes.

The two years have passed pleasantly, happily even, and quickly for Jewel. She is now looking forward to and making plans for graduation. She has applied for and been accepted by the four-year college which is less than thirty minutes from where she and her parents live. She has recently learned that she can graduate from the university in less than two years, if she attends summer school.

From time to time Jewel sees Steven as he passes in his truck. She used to stand at her window and watch for it, *but those days are long gone.* She now has a whole, new life; she feels like a different person. It is getting increasingly difficult for her to recall the sad, depressed young woman who returned to her parents' home following the miscarriage Her parents are delighted with the changes they see in her.

As a computer science major, Jewel has to complete an internship. She is placed with one of the nation's major trucking companies. During her first week on the job, she has learned that Steven's name is included on her computer-generated list, along with the route to which he has been assigned. She also knows that each driver must appear in person to collect his paycheck, unless he has direct deposit.

When Steven comes in for his paycheck, he is very surprised to see Jewel at the computer terminal. She is dressed in a conservative business suit, and looks exactly like what she is: *an up and coming, young professional woman who is very definitely on the move.* Because this is so, at first Steven isn't sure that it is she. But when she looks directly at him and nods a greeting, of course he recognizes her. *God, she looks great,* is his immediate thought. *I'd sure like to have her back,* he realizes, as he exits the building.

At this point, Steven does not know that Jewel has been attending college. He has heard nothing from Jewel, nor of what she has been doing with her life, since their divorce. Because he knows her family well, and was frequently in her home when the two of them were in high school, he has felt too ashamed of what he did to show up in her neighborhood. He acknowledges to himself that *Jewel's parents treated him as an adored son during the period when he and Jewel were married, inviting him to their family reunions, and family-favorite vacation spots, gratis*; he knows how much they love Jewel, their only child, and how pleased they were when they learned of the expected grandchild. He knows that what he did was unconscionable, that it is probably why Jewel lost their baby, and so he has avoided showing his face in her neighborhood, where he used to hang out every chance he got.

The woman with whom he fathered the child, a boy they named Steve, was already married when he met her. Eventually she and her husband reconciled, so he has not seen her, nor the child, for more than two years now.

Since encountering Jewel at the trucking company's main headquarters, he has been unable to get her out of his mind. He begins to ask around and learns about her graduation from the community college, and about her imminent graduation from the university. Steven is astounded. *No wonder she was at that computer terminal dressed so conservatively,* he says to himself. *But Jewel was never interested in college when we were dating; she wasn't even interested in high school,* he recalls.

He is consumed with thoughts of her; he can't get the sight of that pretty face and trim body in that pretty, red suit out of his mind. But he is reluctant to approach her, afraid of rejection. A few days later he sees Jewel and a couple of her colleagues going into the mall. They are headed to the studio that has been commissioned to take pictures of the university graduates this year in their caps and gowns. Jewel does not see him, but he thinks that she does, that she's just ignoring him.

As Jewel and her friends continue on their way up the escalator, Steven sits down on a bench which gives him a view of several of the mall's entrances and exits.

About half an hour later, Jewel and her friends come out of the studio, stop briefly for drinks at one of the food courts they passed going in, and head for the parking lot where they left Jewel's little red Honda. As they walk past the bench where Steven has strategically placed himself, Steven stands up and waves saying, "Hello, how are you?"

"Fine," Jewel says, without missing a step.

"Who was that?" Amber, one of the friends asks. Steven hears this question, but he doesn't hear Jewel's response, since they are continuing to walk. But he does hear the laughter which they share as they continue on their way.

I wonder what she said, he is thinking. *Who did she tell them I am? What's so funny?* All of these questions pass through Steven's mind as he walks toward his car. He is also *wondering if he should call her; if he dares.*

"Hey Man," Owen, one of the other truckers with whom Steven has worked for years says to him a few days later, "Isn't that *fox* who runs the computer your ex? I hear she's graduating from University next week, with honors. I was asking around, trying to find out who she is, if I had a chance, you know, and Sam says she's your ex. Why'd you ever let a *fox* like that get away?" Steven murmurs something indecipherable as he hurries and gets into his truck. But he has been asking himself that same question, ever since he saw Jewel at the computer terminal more than a week ago. *How did I let a fox like that get away? And just what the hell did Owen mean by wondering if he has a chance!* he asks himself.

Although Jewel has finished all of her exams and is currently working full-time for the trucking company, months before her scheduled graduation date, she submitted applications to several large computer firms. She has just been offered a job, a very lucrative one with excellent growth potential, in another state. She plans to take it, and has notified the company of her intentions. When Steven finally gets up the nerve to call her, she says in response to his inquiry, "Steven, I'm *certainly not interested in getting back together.* As much as it hurt when it happened, you actually did me a favor, so I owe you a debt of gratitude. *Thanks*! I'll be moving out-of-state soon. Good-bye."

Steven stands there with the phone, mouth gaping, for a full minute before he recovers the presence of mind to hang it up. He knows that he has lost *a good thing.* He realizes that he and Jewel could have traveled the road to college together, that her parents were the kind of people who would have joyfully helped them both down that path, if he had done things right. He recognizes that Jewel is one Black woman for whom *the yield* was merely a catalyst to a better life, *a life he could have shared.*

Chapter XIII

Sue and No-Commitment Phil

Phil has called Sue several times since their break, wanting to know if she'd like to go out to dinner or to a show, but each time Sue has declined. It is hard for her. Sue has been out of circulation for more than ten years. A lot of things have changed since she was last part of the dating scene, and she is determined never again to get involved in another dead-end relationship.

Six months have gone by since Sue and Phil parted company. During that time, Phil and his brother, Ben, have pooled their resources and have purchased a townhouse. Both of them live in it and share living expenses. Each of them, for short periods of time, has had women move in with them. But at the present time, neither of them does.

This morning as they dress for work, Phil says to Ben, "You know, I *miss* Sue. She's a good woman, nothing anything like the ones I've been involved with lately."

"Then why don't you marry her? She's still free, isn't she?" Ben asks.

"I've got me some living to do first. I'm too young to get married," Phil tells him, more to convince himself than his brother. "I haven't even reached my prime yet, Man. I need to live a little!" he says as he snaps his fingers.

"Then go for it. Live a little, live a lot! But stop talking about how much you miss Sue and get on with the living," Ben tells him.

To this Phil does not respond, but he is realizing, increasingly, that *he does miss Sue, that if the price of having her in his life is marriage, then maybe he should marry her.* Heretofore, he's admitted this to no one, not even to himself. However, he has always thought that *marriage meant that a man was giving up his freedom.* He never thought in terms of freedom being relative. He never recognized before that one aspect of freedom allows that a man is in a position to share his life with whomever he chooses. Well, he recognizes it now, and *Sue is the woman with whom he wants to be.* He has finally admitted this to himself, and now he has made the decision to admit it to her.

A few days later, he calls Sue at work. He knows her work schedule, so he knows that she will probably be at her desk eating lunch, usually an apple, unless she drove over to a nearby mall, which she does occasionally during her lunch hour. "Sue, it's Phil," he says. "Will you marry me?"

"What did you say?" Sue asks.

"You heard me. Will you marry me?" he repeats.

Later that day, Sue allows Phil to drive her home from work. As they drive, she tells him that it's too soon, that they have been separated for the better part of a year. "I don't know what you did during that time, or with whom you've been involved. You should have an AIDS test." She goes on to say, "I've been celibate since we broke up, but I'll take the test too. Let's take it together. *And they do.*

As they await their test results, which will take days, Phil is real apprehensive. *He had not even considered the possibility that he might have been intimate with someone who has been exposed.* But he is fortunate, very fortunate. Both his and Sue's test results are negative. He can feel himself exhale; he breathes deeply for the first time since Sue suggested the test. It has been hell trying to keep her from knowing just how apprehensive and anxious he has been awaiting the results. He knows her well, so he is aware that she is attuned to the slightest changes in his moods. Sometimes he has felt that she could read his thoughts.

"Now will you marry me," he asks.

"Ask me again," she says. "Get down on your knees and ask me." And he does, right there in the doctor's office, oblivious to the three or four other patients waiting there. They look intently at the pair, but the two of them have eyes for one another only. They all smile, listening intently.

Two weeks later, they become husband and wife. Phil wants to resume right where they left off, but Sue is more mature, *and wiser* this time around. She insists upon remaining celibate until they say their vows. Phil respects this, even though he doesn't really like it and had not expected it.

Book II - Yield

Teal

Cookie's garden is spectacular with red, yellow and white roses, fiscus, tulips, and a host of other intoxicating flowers, *all in full bloom*. Tables with white linen cloths have been set up by caterers for the reception which follows the brief ceremony. Dozens of red roses create exquisite centerpieces for each table. Both the bride and the groom are radiant, her smile regal, his equally beautific, proving indeed that happiness for the Black man is possible when he is willing to forsake *the yield*.

Amanda, Gloria, and Hubert-the-Trapped

Gloria is getting angrier by the second. It is now close to midnight and Hubert has not yet arrived, nor has he called. Gloria has been chain-smoking for the past two hours; now she says to herself, *"I'll give him five more minutes; if he isn't here, I'm calling his home, damnit!*

Meanwhile, Hubert says to his wife, "Do you think I should drive over there?"

"Hubert, at this hour the company is closed; you know that. The emergency answering service has to reach one of their on-call repairmen. That's the only way anybody can arrange for emergency service at this late hour," Amanda tells him.

Hubert's wife has always taken care of family emergencies in the past. Most of them have taken place while Hubert was at work, or elsewhere, never before on a Friday night well past midnight. He really does not know much about handling family emergencies, but he does know that a heating company is not likely to be open at this hour. Still he says, "Well, the Yellow Pages Directory said twenty-four hour service, day or night."

"I know that," Amanda says, "but that still doesn't mean that there is someone on-site at the company at all times."

Hubert makes no oral response to Amanda's remarks, but he is still *wondering how he can get away so he can get a message to Gloria.* He says, "I'm going out for cigarettes. This waiting is getting to me. Do you need anything from the store?"

Book II - Yield

Teal

"Hubert, I'd rather you didn't. If no one from the company returns our call soon, we're going to have to take the kids to a hotel to spend the night. We can't spend the night here under these circumstances," Amanda says.

"I agree, but I still don't see how my running out to the store will preclude any of that," he says.

"It won't," Amanda tells him, "but I just feel better with you here. Lil' Huey already has a terrible cold, and I'm not going to let him sleep here in this frigid house much longer. If we go to a hotel, you can get cigarettes in the lobby there. If it's all the same to you, I'd rather you just wait."

Well, it's not all the same to Hubert. *He needs to get to a phone; he needs to get a message to Gloria.* As he is thinking this, the phone rings. "Thank God!" Amanda says, *believing it to be the call for which they have been waiting.* Hubert grabs the phone.

Without preamble Gloria says, "Hubert, do you know what the fucking time is?" As Hubert is *wondering how he is going to be able to respond to this conversation,* Lil' Huey starts to cough. Amanda heads in the direction of the cough.

As soon as Amanda is out of hearing range, Hubert begins, "I'm terribly sorry, but I'm going to have to cancel tonight. It can't be helped. I'll explain to you later." Following this, he hangs up before Gloria has a chance to respond.

Gloria is livid! She can't believe he hung up on her. She can't believe he's allowed something else to take precedence over spending time with her, over taking her to this once-a-year affair. He knows how much this means to her.

Gloria, like many women who are having affairs with married men, believes herself to be more important to him than she is. She sincerely does not believe that primarily what she is to him is a willing sex partner from whom he can get it free of charge, but that his emotions, his vigilance, are usually reserved for his family. While she deludes herself that she is the object of his affections, as he is of hers, the reality is that she is his disposable plaything, an object of his sexual desire, and that's only if it comes in the *trouble free, no-strings-attached variety.* In short, she allows herself to be duped as well as used.

Coming back into the room, Amanda asks, "Are they on their way?"

"Who?" questions Hubert. For a moment he has *actually forgotten.* As Amanda gives him a strange look he says, "Just kidding. No, they're not on the way, but someone from the company should be contacting us any minute now." While he is saying this, the phone rings again. Fearing that it is Gloria calling back, Hubert grabs the phone but is relieved to find that it is the call for which they've been waiting. A repairman has been dispatched and should be at their home within the hour.

The following Monday Hubert is at his desk thirty minutes early. As soon as he arrives, he phones Gloria. He explains about the heating problem; he apologizes about the ball...

Gloria is not appeased. She spent hundreds of dollars for her dress, her manicure, her hairdo; *all for naught*! Several of her coworkers have already stopped by her desk inquiring about her absence from the ball. Never before has she missed the company's annual ball, not once since she started working for the company nearly ten years ago. She feels not just angry, but humiliated. She has bragged to several of her female coworkers who are also involved with married men, "He's mine tonight!" in reference to her and Hubert's date for the ball, and so she is in no mood to hear about his family being the reason he stood her up. He knew she'd spent hundreds of dollars for her own attire; that she'd also rented formal attire for him which also cost hundreds of dollars. As far as she is concerned, standing her up is inexcusable.

She tells Hubert, in no uncertain terms, that she does not accept his apology. Practically shouting into the phone she says, "If your family is going to cause me problems like this, or any kinds of problems for that matter, either you get rid of them, or I'll get rid of you!"

In response to this Hubert says, "Do whatever you have to do, Gloria." Though he is in hot pursuit of, and still deeply attracted by *the yield*, he is not willing to give up his family for it.

Ruth, Josh, and Maybe Dexter

Dexter, the principal of an elementary school in a Denver surburb, is a busy man. Ruth understands this, yet when he has to cancel or delay a date for any reason, she wonders if he is being honest with her; if his reasons are legitimate ones, the ones he's given to her. Frequently her thoughts return *to Josh, the deception, the years of lying and pretending, the years of hoping and dreaming, planning and internalizing.* She still has trouble believing how clueless she was. *She and Josh dated for more than three years, to the exclusion of anyone else,* she believed. Now she feels like a complete fool, as if there was probably something which would have alerted her if she had been intelligent enough to detect it.

Did she let her heart overrule her common sense? she frequently asks herself. She has even asked this question of her best friends, two other young women with whom she shared dorm rooms during her freshmen and junior years at college. Both Rita and Janet have told her that they too were clueless, that Dexter behaved as if he were a single man, that he acted just like the vast majority of all the other male students at their university: he hung around their dorms like a love-sick puppy, he held her hand whenever they walked together across the campus, he bought her gifts for all of the holidays, he escorted her to all of the campus affairs which they both attended. *So what was she supposed to think?* they've asked her.

"He never invited me to meet his parents," she's told them, and they've explained to her that there's nothing unusual about that, that plenty of girls dated guys on the campus to whom their parents were never introduced, or conversely.

"I know that," Ruth told them, "but how many of the girls on campus dated a guy for three whole years, *almost four*, and never met either of his parents, at least once? Tell me that!" she said, practically hysterically.

To this Rita responds, "Ruth, everybody has twenty/twenty hindsight! Of course in retrospect you'd realize there's something suspiciously secretive about that. Who wouldn't? But during the years when Josh ran his great scam, he acted completely natural, as far as any of us could tell, so it wasn't you only who got deceived, Joshua deceived all of us!"

"And I don't appreciate the fact that all of his homeboys went right along with the deception. Some of them *had* to know that Josh was married. Not once did any of them ever give any intimation that this was so. Those guys must be conscienceless!"

"I don't think they're conscienceless," Ruth tells them. "I think it was all a big game to them, and being members of that tacit brotherhood, *the old boys' network*, the unspoken agreement is always in effect: *you don't rat on a brother, you mind your own business when it comes to another man's business with his woman, or women.* We all know how it is, but since we'd never think of treating anyone as shabbily as they obviously are capable of treating others, we just can't think like they do."

Meanwhile, Ruth and Dexter are becoming serious. She decides to share her feelings of hurt and betrayal with him; she wants him to understand why she is so often suspicious of his motives.

Dexter is understanding, but he makes it clear that he does not want to be compared with Josh or with anyone else, for that matter. He tells her that he is his own man, and that he has nothing, whatsoever, to do with the other guys she has known and interacted with in her past. "I know that each of us is impacted, and to a certain extent shaped, by our individual experiences," he tells her, "but we do not have to allow those experiences, however unpleasant they may have been, to dictate our future reactions to others. I believe everybody should be judged on his or her own merit. Don't assume I'm a liar because *that guy* was a liar. I'd never hoodwink a Black woman. My mother and sister, both of whom I lover dearly, are Black women. Both of them raised me because my father died when I was just two, and my sister is almost twelve years older than I am. I respect Black women. Give me a chance; I'll be straight with you, as I'll expect you to be with me. I'm in no hurry. Let's take it nice and slow, and see what develops," he says.

Ruth is impressed by Dexter's straightfowardness. She promises herself *to give him the chance he says he wants*. Her intentions are sincere, but as time passes, she finds it impossible to be trusting. She can't forget what being trusting once got her, and so still, every time Dexter has to cancel a date or is delayed for any reason, *she doubts his sincerity, his truthfulness*. Even when she promises herself that she isn't going to verbalize her feelings about these doubts, she finds herself alluding to them in Dexter's presence. Dexter is a good man; his intentions are entirely honorable, but Ruth has been permanently scarred by *the yield*.

Chapter XIV

Ida and Disappearing Sydney

Ida's parents are really concerned for her. She won't eat, she has trouble sleeping, and she has missed three consecutive days of school. It is now a Friday evening and Nora, Ida's mom says, "If you're feeling no better by Monday, I'm taking you to the doctor. Ida, won't you please tell us what the problem is?" But Ida says nothing.

Ida is now in her room lying across her bed. Her mind is on Sydney. She is *wondering if Sydney had some emergency and will soon contact her to explain why he moved so suddenly.* She still has not allowed herself to accept that he would run out on her believing her to be carrying his child. Everything she has been taught rebels against the notion that one human being would do that to another, that a man who has spent months professing his love for her and his desire to be with her, would just cut out, disappear, because he thinks that a child which he has fathered is on the way.

The following Monday, Ida goes back to school. Since this is her junior year and she is the student government representative for her class, she does not want to miss the meeting which is scheduled after school today. This meeting's agenda includes plans for the junior prom. She wants to be a part of this discussion.

Immediately following dismissal from school today, members of the student council have gathered for their monthly meeting. While these students are waiting for their teacher sponser to arrive so the meeting can begin, Lucas asks Ida if she already has a date for the prom. Simone, who has been hoping that Lucas will invite her to be his date for the prom does not give Ida a chance to respond. She cuts in and says, "Ida's probably coming to the prom with Sidney. Aren't you, Ida?"

"Sydney moved back to his hometown. He's been gone for weeks now. I thought everybody knew," Ida says. Before anyone else has a chance to respond, Mr. Delille arrives, signals the student government president to call the meeting to order; the gavel is sounded and the meeting begins.

During the school day, Ida is able to almost forget about Sydney, but the conversation right before the meeting set her to thinking about him again. Now, as she walks home with a group of other junior girls, she is trying to remember *if Sydney ever mentioned where his family lives. He must have*, she says to herself, *but I can't remember where he said he was from. I know what I'll do. I'll call the maintenance company where he worked. Surely they'll know where he's from, and maybe where he went even. They might've transferred him to another one of their offices.*

When Ida calls, she learns that the company has no idea where Sydney went, nor why he left the company so suddenly, but they do know that he started with the company right after he finished high school in Memphis. As she is hearing this, she begins thinking about her Aunt Helen, her mother's only sister, who lives in Memphis. She used to visit with her for a week every summer when she was a little girl. *I'm going to ask Mom if I can visit Aunt Helen this summer,* she says to herself.

That summer, almost as soon as school lets out, Ida is on the train to Memphis to spend a week with her Aunt Helen. While she is there, *she learns that two of Sydney's previous girlfriends have babies which he fathered, that he married neither of them, and that he denied paternity in both cases. She also learns that he did return to Memphis briefly after leaving Biloxi, but no one seems to know where he is currently.*

Ida considers herself lucky indeed. As she nears the completion of her senior year and makes plan for entering college in the fall, she has all but forgotten the pain she felt when she learned of Sydney's defection. From time to time *she remembers her parents saying to her, "But we don't know a thing about this Sydney,"* and how, at the time, she had honestly felt that they knew enough about him, all they needed to know. She has grown up a lot; *she now realizes that it is foolish to believe, to just accept at face value, what a total stranger tells her.* She also realizes that *that's* what Sydney was to her: *a total stranger.* This experience has matured her beyond her years. Ida knows how fortunate she is that she didn't become another disposable pawn in Sydney's chess game where only willing females are the pawns, and that *the yield* didn't checkmate her.

Wilber, Ester, and Daughter, Queen

Wilber left that night with only the clothes on his back. He went directly to an old girlfriend's house. He told her that he and Ester were having problems and that he'd left her. "Is it okay if I spend the night on your sofa?" he asks.

"You don't have to sleep on the sofa, Baby. Sounds like you could use some comfort,' Connie says, reaching to give Wilber a hug. Wilber stands there and allows her to embrace him, but he doesn't return the embrace. He is in no mood for Connie's brand of comfort. He feels terrible about what has happened, worse than he could have possibly imagined.

Meanwhile, back at the house Queen is crying as she tells her mother about the nice restaurant to which Wilber took her for dinner, the glass of wine he allowed her to have. "I'm so sorry, Mom," Queen says. "I didn't mean to do anything wrong. Honest I didn't."

Ester comforts her. "Of course you didn't, Baby. Nothing here that happened is your fault. I don't blame you for anything, and I don't want you blaming yourself for any of this. You hear me?"

"Are you going to let him come back?" Queen asks. I like him Mom, He's never done anything like this before."

"And he's not going to have the chance to do anything like it again, not with my daughter anyhow. No, he's not coming back here. Even before this happened, I had started to suspect that Wilber was doing some things that were not right, *but I don't want to get into that*. This is our home, and it's my responsibility to make sure that you're safe in it. I've always done that, and as long as you're my daughter, I intend to do that. I can't work unless I know that you're safe, *and I have to work.* You understand that, don't you?"

"Yes, Mom, I know that you have to work to take care of us, and I am sorry all of this happened. I didn't mean to cause trouble between you and Wilber."

"Stop saying that; stop thinking that. Didn't I tell you that you're not to blame for any of this, and that I don't want you to blame yourself. You didn't cause the trouble between us; he did. I want you to understand that. You did nothing wrong," Ester says as she hugs Queen. "Now go on and get ready for bed. After you get your pajamas on, come into the kitchen. I'll make hot chocolate for the two of us. Would you like that?" Ester asks as she leaves Queen's bedroom.

The following morning, which is a Saturday, Wilber is gone before Connie awakens. He had thought about it the night before and meant to be gone before Connie awakened. He does not want to talk with Connie about his family situation, and he does consider Ester and Queen his family.

He goes to a coffee shop and sits in a corner booth smoking one cigarette after another. The waitress asks for the third time if he is ready to order now. "Bring me a pot of coffee," he says irritably. He has never felt this miserable in his life. *What was I thinking of?* he asks himself repeatedly. *I can't believe I made a play for Ester's little girl. I wouldn't have done anything to her, I know I wouldn't.* All of this keeps going through Wilber's mind as he sits there, staring at nothing, but seeing everything: *he sees Queen sprinting up the stairs to get dressed for dinner. He sees the look of astonishment on her face when he allows her to order a glass of wine. He sees her running into the bathroom and locking the door when she realizes he's taken the towel.* For the first time, he allows himself a clear glimpse into his true character and the mental image is grotesque.

When Wilber leaves the restaurant, he drives past the house that was his home *three times*, but he can't get up the nerve to go in. Later that morning he calls Ester, using the mobile phone that was Queen's and Ester's Christmas gift to him. He asks, "Can I come by to talk with you?"

In response Ester says, "What is there to talk about? I know what you did; you know what you did. I could, and would, never trust you again in the same room, unsupervised, with my child. So you tell me, what is there to say?"

Wilber has no response. What can he say? *He realizes that he's lost his family. He realizes that he cares more for Ester than he thought.* He would like to have her back, but his quest for *the yield* has cost him her love and respect.

Book II - Yield

Sheena, Boyd, and Liz

Sheena decides that she must change her church membership. She tells her good friend, Doris, "I can't sit and listen to Boyd Sunday after Sunday up there sounding so earnest, knowing what he did, knowing that he preaches one way of life, but lives another. I always believed that preachers practiced what they preached."

"Sheena, I think most of them do, or at least they try to," Doris says in response. "But they're just people too. Now don't get me wrong, I also expect a preacherman, and preacherwoman too for that matter, to live what he or she preaches, but let's be realistic. How many of us, preacher or not, are really able to do what the Good Book recommends, all the time? God knows some of us try harder than others, but not too many of us make it, if truth be told."

Doris tries to convince Sheena to stay, not to change her membership. The two of them grew up in that church, singing in youth choirs, saying Easter speeches; participating in Christmas pagents, and more. They attended the same Sunday School class; went to the same Vacation Bible School for years. Sheena is torn. She has so many friends, so much history that is important to her here at this church, and she does feel the need to be surrounded by her friends more than ever now. But at the same time, she doesn't welcome their unctuous sentiments. She just likes the camaraderie, the sense of belonging that she feels when she is among them.

Book II - Yield

Teal

For the next several Sundays, Sheena visits other local churches, but she is not inspired to join either of them. As she sat and listened to each of the sermons, her focus was only partially on the words being spoken. Intermittently, *her mind would wander back to Boyd's about face, his betrayal, his escalating absences away from home; his refusal to include her in his ministerial life.*

The next Sunday, she returns to her own church. As she enters the sanctuary, a bit later than her usual arrival time, Boyd is already in the pulpit preaching. His sermon is entitled, *Learning How to Forgive.* As Sheena listens, she is thinking, *I wonder if he has forgiven himself. I wonder if he realizes what he has done to me. She makes an instant decision: I'm going to ask him.*

Following the benediction, Boyd stands at the entrance, shaking hands with members and visitors as they leave the sanctuary. Sheena waits until all of the others are gone, then she walks up to Boyd, reaches for his hand and says, "Boyd, I'd like to have a word with you. Can I see you in your office for a few minutes?" Boyd feels somewhat apprehensive, but he proceeds to the office. On his desk there is still the wedding snapshot which was his favorite of the lot. Sheena framed it for him during their honeymoon. This surprises Sheena. *She thought he would have gotten rid of it by now; it has been several months since she moved out of the parsonage.*

Without preamble Sheena says, "Boyd, tell me why during the two years in which we dated, you always made time for me in your life, but shortly after the marriage there never seemed to be any time for me?"

Boyd denies that this was so. "You know I'm a busy man," he says. "I have responsibilities; you knew that before we were married. I don't know why you gave me so little understanding after we were married. I wouldn't have asked you to be my wife if I hadn't wanted to be married to you."

Sheena is surprised to hear Boyd speak this way. He has completely discounted the affair with Liz. He is talking as if their only problem was *her attitude. She begins to wonder if Boyd is aware that she knew of the affair with Liz.* She says, "What about Liz?"

"What about her?" he asks.

"You know what I'm asking, Boyd," she says quietly. But Boyd insists he doesn't know what she's talking about. He maintains that he and Liz spent time together strictly because of their work. He is not willing to be honest about the brief affair he had with her. He won't admit, not even to himself, that he had an affair with Liz during his brief marriage to Sheena.

Though the affair was short-lived and lacked substance, nevertheless, it did happen, and Sheena, as well as a few of the other members, are aware that it happened.

Boyd, like some other preachers, preaches morality. But he does not practice it, not when it conflicts with his sexual desires. He wants to do what is right, and most of the time he does. But for Boyd, *the yield* has an attraction far more compelling than the truth of his scriptures.

Chapter XV

Erica, Sam, and His Need for Freedom

When Sam arrives home well past midnight, he is unaware that the girls are there, asleep in their old room. He gets into bed, sleeping with his back to Erica. He keeps as far away from her as he can in the king-sized bed. He has no need, sexually, for his wife. He has only minutes ago come from Keri's bed.

Before he awakens the next morning, Eri is up and in the kitchen. She has not slept well. Without Eri's knowledge, both of the girls attack Sam at once. They go into the master suite, wake him up, and Dawn, the more outspoken of the two girls says, "What do you mean you need your freedom? You're an old man. You need freedom for what?"

Book II - Yield

Teal

Sam is still groggy from sleep. *He had no idea the girls were there; he had no idea they knew anything about this. He had counted on Eri's discretion, her love for them, her protectiveness of them, and her need for privacy, to protect him. He had not even considered the possibility that she would tell them, especially before the divorce was a foregone conclusion. And in his mind, it is not a foregone conclusion.* Even though he has whored around throughout the marriage, *he knows his wife to be the stablizing force in his life; his family to be his link to decency and acceptance in circles he respects, and he has no desire to lose that.* But neither does he have any desire to change his immoral behavior.

Stalling for time he says, "How about you girls letting your old man get dressed. Then we'll talk more."

But Dawn is having none of it. She is enraged! "Why do you need to get dressed to tell us why you need your freedom? What do you plan to do with your freedom?" she asks heatedly.

Stuttering now: "You-you girls can-can't poss-possibly un-understand this. It has-has nothing to-to do wi-with you. This-this is be-between your mother an-and me," Sam says.

"The hell it is!" Dawn says. "You've always said that we're a family. Now you tell us why you need your freedom! Does that mean we're no longer a family, that you now want to be free of us? Is that the message?"

Sam has never been able to stand up under the girls' scrutiny. Now he *feels caged, entrapped. He is not prepared to discuss this with the girls; he feels as though they are forcing his hand.* He says, "Your mother shouldn't have mentioned this to you. She and I have not yet ironed it out. I don't know why she'd trouble you with our problems."

Diedra cuts in with, "Do you really believe Mom could have a problem that wouldn't cause us to have a problem also? If you do, you're not the dad you raised us to believe you are." *This cuts Sam to the quick.* He's always been proud of what he instilled in his girls, and of how he *knew* they felt about him. "Let me get this straight. So what you're telling us, in effect, is that you expected her to suffer silently, to protect your good name; your good image, right?" Diedra says passionately.

Until this very moment, Sam has not thought of it in these terms. But the girls have always been capable of forcing him to make a *reality check. And this is exactly what he has expected.* Of course he can't admit that to the girls, so he says instead, "What I ex-expected is that she and I wou-wou-would first decide exactly what our course of action wou-wou-would be before discus-discussing the situation with you-you girls, or anyone else for that matter."

But the girls are not having it. They are fuming about the fact that he would hurt their mother, threaten her sense of well-being. Everything he's taught them is at stake if he can do this. They are not nearly ready to let him off the hook. "If that's the case," Dawn says, "why didn't you iron it out before mentioning your need for freedom to Mother? Why are you allowed to mention it to her before it's all ironed out, but she isn't allowed to mention it to us? *You're full of it, Dad!"*

Neither of his girls has ever spoken disrespectfully to Sam before. *He feels like crying, and he knows that he is in no position to reprimand them.*

At this point Erica hears Dawn's voice, which has risen considerably since the conversation began. As she enters the bedroom she says, "What on earth...?" She realizes the girls must have awakened Sam and are attacking him about his need for freedom. She had not expected this; had not wanted it. *In fact, she had intended to ask them not to mention anything about this to him.* But she can see it's too late for that now. "Girls, girls," she says, "please come into the kitchen. Breakfast is ready. Now is not the time for this."

But the girls are angry; their sense of justice, of fair-play, has been violated. They are nowhere close to consumating this discussion."But Mom," Dawn says, "he can't just put you aside like an old piece of outdated Samsonite that he no longer needs or wants! If he doesn't want you, then we don't want him. It's as simple as that! We're a family; that's what he always said. It's either true or it isn't. He never said we're a family as long as it suits him. He said we're a family. Period. Didn't he always say that? Whenever Diedra and I used to fight, he'd make us kiss and make up, and he'd say, 'you're family and family members don't fight. They love each other; they talk it out and make peace.' What happened to that? Does that just apply to Diedra and me but not to you and him?"

Sam has escaped into the bathroom as the last of this is being said. Erica has finally persuaded the girls to follow her into the kitchen. In there she says to them, "Girls, I know how you feel. I've felt what you're feeling, and more, but Sam has to make his own decisions. You girls could probably persuade him to do the right thing, but if he does the right thing, I need to know that it's his decision. If he has a need for freedom, and if what we already share does not represent freedom for him, if he's feeling smothered by our family, then maybe he shouldn't be a part of it any longer. Sam will always be your dad; that's not optional. But whether or not he remains a part of this family unit is optional. Please, please, drop this. Please. Erica is obviously quite distressed. Seeing her anguish, the girls drop it. Reluctantly. They follow their mom into the kitchen and sit at the table in the places where they sat as little girls, as teenagers; now as young women. Neither of them says a word; both are *thinking of all the pleasant times, the conversations, the love and peace and happiness they experienced at that table, with both their parents basking in their presence, in the knowledge that they were privileged to have the two of them, and making no secret of how they felt about the fact.*

In the bathroom, Sam is sweating. He certainly had not counted on such rude awakening. He is *wondering how he can avoid eating breakfast with the family. He feels ill, that he can't handle anymore just now. He wishes he could start all over again; that he could be true to his wife and to the ideals he planted in the hearts of his girls. He wishes his girls knew only positive things about him, that his image was still untarnished in their minds.* He has a deep, psychological need for this to be so, but that is no longer possible. They will never feel and think about him as they did before any of this happened, before they knew anything about all of this. He has lost their respect, if not their love. It has been displaced by his attachment to *the yield*.

Book II - Yield

Teal

Eunice and Eugene, the Weekend Alcoholic

Erin has been sneaking beer for more than a year now. Sometimes when he gets his allowance, he gets an older friend to buy beer for him. For the past four months he has been sneaking some of the stronger stuff: a little bourbon, a little whiskey; a little gin. His dad's never missed it. Recently, emboldened by the alcohol, Erin has been thinking: *and so what if he does, he drinks a lot more than I do.*

Erin's English teacher *has suspected that he has come to class under the influence.* "Have you noticed Erin Stanford's eyes lately? They're awfully bright. Do you think he's on something?" she asks a coworker.

"I haven't, but that doesn't mean that he isn't. It's just that my class which Erin attends is so large, over thirty students, so I don't have much time for noticing things like students' eyes. I'm too busy trying to keep control of the group as a whole, so my attention is focused there," he says.

"I know what you mean," Maxine says. "I have that same problem in two of my own classes."

Meanwhile, Erin is getting bolder at home. He's sneaking more and more of Eugene's *beverages.* But since Eugene doesn't normally see what's left from one weekend to the next, he just doesn't notice.

Eunice is cleaning Erin and Bary's room. As she cleans, she is putting their dirty laundry into a pile outside of the bedroom door in the hallway. Leaving the room, she picks up the dirty laundry. There is, unmistakably the smell of whiskey. She's troubled by this smell, and thoroughly familiar with it from years of smelling in on her husband's breath and clothing.

In the kitchen, she shakes each item of clothing individually, and sniffs it. The smell is emanating from Erin's favorite sweatshirt. There is a wide spill directly down the front of it. *Eunice wonders how it got there. I'll have to ask him about that,* she says to herself, as she loads the washer.

When Erin comes home from school that day, Eunice says to him, "Erin, there is a stain down the front of you Cowboys sweatshirt, the blue one that you wear all the time. What is that stain?" She doesn't want Erin to know that she has washed the sweatshirt. In fact, *she is thinking that she should not have washed it until after this conversation.*

"I have no idea, Mom. What does it look like?" he asks. *But he does know what it is*; he remembers the spill. He was sneaking a drink of whiskey when he thought he heard someone coming; that's when he spilled it on his shirt. It turned out to be their dog, Curly, but he got quite a scare. He had meant to put the sweatshirt in the washer himself, but Erin is not a neat guy, he doesn't usually wash his own clothes, so he just forgot about it. Now *he is hoping that his mom will do the same, and just drop this subject.* But he is out of luck. Eunice is *very attuned* to anything alcoholic. She has been trying, for years, to get Eugene to attend A.A. Meetings, so there's no way she's going to forget about that smell, that stain. She does, however, decide to say no more about it just then.

But what she does decide to do is to mark the level of each bottle of alcohol every Sunday night, and to count the cans of beer that are left in the refrigerator every Sunday night. It doesn't take long for her to confirm that someone else in their home is drinking beer and alcohol besides Eugene. *She determines to find out who it is.* Now, whenever she hears the refrigerator door open and/or close, she goes into the kitchen.

She moves the ironing board from the guest bedroom where she's always kept it into the kitchen, so that as she presses their clothes, she can see who uses the refrigerator and for what. She moves the bottles of alcohol from the lowest to the highest pantry shelf, and pushes them into the back. In front of them she stacks canned goods so that the children no longer know where they are and it isn't obvious that they are on the topmost shelf. If they learn, a ladder or chair will be required to gain access to what is stored on that shelf. Except for alerting Eugene and explaining her reasons to him, she says nothing about these changes to anyone.

Erin has looked and discovered that the alcoholic beverages are no longer stored where they've been stored for as long as he can remember, long before he even thought about sneaking them. *He wonders where they are now, but he can't ask.* He is feeling the need, increasingly, for more and more alcohol. He has played hooky from school a couple of times with other boys to go to a drinking party. He has taken money from his mother's purse to buy beer. *His desire for alcohol is getting out of control, but he isn't aware that this is so.*

This is a Saturday night and Eugene and his drinking buddies are in the backyard playing dominoes. They have a case of beer on ice, and a variety of other kinds of alcoholic beverages in a cooler hidden from *busybodies*. Erin is wondering how he can get some. He is really feeling the need for it. When he was little, his dad would often give him a taste of the beer he was drinking. *He is wondering if he goes out there now, will he be offered a taste.* But he is reluctant. Usually, when his dad is drinking, he is mean;

unreasonable, so his kids try to stay out of his path. But Erin's need has become stronger than his fear. He goes out and sits on the back step; he sits there for several minutes. When his dad doesn't notice him or say anything to him, he walks over to the table and says, "Dad, can I have a sip of your beer?"

Eugene is surprised, a little startled even, by this. Eunice has told him about her suspicions, and even though he gave no credence to the story at the time, he has not forgotten about it. "Boy," he says menancingly, "have you been drinking my liquor?"

Now Erin wishes he had stayed away from his dad, just as he usually does when he is drinking. *He knows that this was an unwise decision,* but his system's demand is greater than his psyche's anxiety. Just the hope of a little taste was motivation enough for him to risk the effort. "No," he replies in a squeaky voice, as he looks down at his feet.

"You look at me, Boy, when you speak to me! Show your old man some respect! I work hard for you kids; I expect to be respected! Is that clear?" Eugene asks.

Erin slinks away. He feels terrible; *he is wondering if his mom will allow him to walk over to his friend's house.* He asks, but she says, "Erin, it's too late for you to be out on the street. It's after nine o'clock. Erin doesn't respond, but he had expected a negative answer from his mom. His mother likes for him and his siblings to be at home at night; she feels more comfortable with all of them in the house. Before Erin began to drink, he accepted this as normal; as the way it should be. But now he resents having such close tabs kept on him. He resents his dad's attitude about a little sip of beer. *What's the big deal?* he says to himself. *He drinks a whole lot more than a sip! He gave me sips when I was just a baby!*

Eunice has been watching Erin closely since the sweatshirt incident. Tonight she notices that he is unusually jumpy. "Is there something going on that you aren't telling me, Erin?" she asks.

"No Mom, I just don't feel too good," he says. She asks what he thinks the matter is, but he says that he doesn't know. Eunice feels nagging doubts. Her mother's intuition tells her that something is amiss. She tells Erin that she is going to make an appointment for his yearly physical sometimes next week, that it will be a little early this year, but that can't hurt. She tells him to go to bed, that maybe he'll feel better in the morning.

Erin feels no better the following morning. Eunice has been keeping such close watch on the refrigerator; she's always in the kitchen now. Erin is beginning to feel withdrawal pains. It's been almost four days since he had anything alcoholic in his system, *and he's feeling it.*

The following week, she tells Erin that she'll be picking him up from school early on Tuesday; she gives him a note to alert the office. She picks him up two hours before dismissal for that day; she takes him for his annual physical.

The doctor is in a long time with Erin. After the physical is complete, he asks Eunice to join him and Erin in his office. He has had a long talk with Erin, who has been his patient since birth. Erin has admitted the drinking to Dr. McCrary. He tells Eunice about it. He also tells her where there is an A.A. Youth Group that meets in the area where she and her family live.

Book II - Yield

Teal

On the way home Eunice says, "Why didn't you tell me? Didn't you think I'd want to help you? Don't you know how much I love you, Erin?"

"Mom, I didn't think it was a problem. I only sneaked little bits at first, then I started sneaking a little more. I'm sorry," he says.

"Erin," she tells him, "sneaking alcohol means you knew it was something you should not have been doing. You don't sneak when you want a coke or some orange juice. Alcohol can be dangerous and it's not meant for growing children. Even adults need to be careful with it. Don't you know that?" she asks. He doesn't say anything. He feels terrible.

"You know that A.A. Group Dr. McCrary told us about. We're going to that meeting tonight, and we're going every week from now on, *every day if we need to*. The doctor says you have a good chance of staying clean and sober if we attend the meetings faithfully. And we will attend them faithfully. I will not allow you to ruin your life with alcohol."

Later that evening when Eugene gets home from work, Eunice tells him all that has transpired between herself and Erin. She tells him what Erin's physical revealed; she tells him about the A.A. Meetings recommended by Dr. McCrary. "The doctor says Erin stands a chance only if the whole family is willing to get involved. Will you go with us to the meetings?" she asks.

Eugene agrees to go with them. He says, "I don't have a drinking problem; I've told you that for years. Just as Erin's physical revealed his drinking problem, some of the ones I've has would've revealed mine, *if I had one*. But I'm certainly willing to do whatever I can to help Erin." Eunice makes no response to this, but she says to herself, *Erin didn't know how to go in and fake it like you know how to do. Erin doesn't know how to lay low for a few days or weeks prior to his physical. Erin isn't able to schedule his own physical, at times opportune to himself.*

Eunice is satisfied with this *for now*. She is hoping that his presence in the meetings will help him with his drinking problem as well, and will perhaps inspire him to attend some of the A.A. Meetings for adult alcoholics, even though he's never admitted that he has a drinking problem. She is optimistic that the meetings will motivate him to realize and accept that he does have a drinking problem and that he will forsake *the yield* for the sake of his son, if not for himself.

Luther, and Lacy. Perfection?

Luther continues to proclaim to his friends that he loves Lacy; that he wants her back. He tells them that he has never, and will never love anyone else.

Lacy has met with him only once since their separation and has told him, in no uncertain terms, that she will not even consider taking him back unless he commits to attending counseling sessions with her, and follows through. Luther does not like the idea, *but he does want his wife back; he agrees to go with her.*

Today is the date of their first scheduled counseling session. Luther has agreed to meet Lacy at the counseling center at 8p.m. for the session which is scheduled from eight to nine o'clock.

Lacy arrives first. She goes into the room where they have agreed to meet and is given a questionnaire by the receptionist. She is asked to respond to the questionnaire while she is waiting for Luther to arrive and for the session to begin. Luther will be asked to respond to an identical questionnaire when he arrives. *But Luther does not arrive.* Lacy waits for him until 8:45, then she apologizes to the receptionist and leaves, telling her that she will call and schedule another appointment, *if Luther agrees.*

As Lacy drives back to her parents' home, which she now shares with them, *she is wondering what happened.* She knows that Luther does not like the idea of going to counseling, but she still *does not believe that he would just stand her up without a word.* As it turns out, Luther had a blowout on the expressway and had been unable to get a message to her. He promised that he would go to the next scheduled session. He told her to go ahead and schedule another session. He said he'd do anything to get her back.

"Why don't you come on back home tonight?" he asks. "We can still go to counseling if that's what you want."

"I'm not doing that, Luther," she tells him. "I made the mistake once of thinking that I knew you because we grew up together, but I quickly learned that I didn't; I still don't. I don't know you at all, and you don't know me either if you think I'd subject myself to the same situation knowingly. You've got some serious problems, and unless you demonstrate that you're willing to deal with them, head on, I'm not taking you back. *I love you*. I've never denied that, and I'm not going to deny it now. I've loved you since we were children. Maybe that's why I was so blind, but that doesn't mean that I can live with you. That's already been proven to my satisfaction, and it should be pretty clear to you by now too."

"I love you too," he acknowledges. "You know I do. We've *both* loved each other since we were kids. Are you telling me that two people who love each other like we do need some *white* counselor in our business before we can live together as man and wife?"

"Luther, I don't want us to live together as *man and wife*. We've already tried that, and it doesn't work for us. In fact, I'm not sure it works for any couple. I want us to live together as *husband and wife,* and there is a difference. You see, *a man* is a noun, *but husband is also a verb*! There's a certain behavior that's expected *and required* of a husband, and you apparently know nothing about that. Well, the only way we're going to get back together is that you learn that expected behavior," Lacy tells him.

"I still don't see why we need some white counselor all in our business before we can get back together," he says.

"Look Luther, if you don't like the counselor I've found, then you find one, a Black one if that's what you want. I don't care what color the counselor is, all I care about is getting the help that's needed." Luther does not respond to this, *but he is still resistant to the idea.*

At the first counseling session, which they attend together, the counselor looks at the responses to their questionnaires before ushering them into her office.

As they wait to be summoned, Luther comments to Lacy, "What're we supposed to do, lay on a sofa and spill our guts?"

"Luther, that sounds like something that might happen in a psychiatrist's office. We're here for marital counseling, remember?" she says.

Before he has a chance to respond, Tonya, the counselor, steps into the waiting area and says," Mr. and Mrs. Warner." They follow her into the inner office where she introduces herself and tells them to call her Tonya. "May I call the two of you by your first names?" she asks. Now she says, "If you're agreeable, I'd like to speak with each of you, individually, for a few minutes. After that, we'll all come back in here and talk together."

Luther doesn't like this idea of separating. For some reason, the idea of talking with the counselor alone frightens him; he feels as if he's choking momentarily; he is almost desperate to escape the office; he feels terrified. His stomach does a few somersaults. He is about to object, but Lacy nudges him with her knee under the table; he remains silent.

Lacy gets up and goes back into the waiting area. Tonya talks privately with Luther first. "Why do you think you and Lacy need a marriage counselor?" she asks. She also asks why they are separated and what he thinks it will take for the two of them to get back together again.

Luther hedges. "I don't think we really need a marriage counselor," he says. "I think the two of us can work it out by ourselves." He tells her that they're separated because they had a few problems. When asked to be more specific, he refuses, saying that they are just problems that any married couple might have. Tonya knows that he is resistant, so she doesn't push at this point; for the most part she listens without comment. As Luther leaves the office, he can feel himself exhale. Tonya hears him too and wonders what his fear is. She tells him to ask Lacy to come in now.

When it is Lacy's turn, she is asked the same questions. She says, "I think we need a marriage counselor because my husband has a problem which he is unwilling, or unable, to face without help." She goes on to say that the two of them are separated because, "Luther wouldn't come home consistently when we were married, and not knowing when he was or was not coming home, made me a nervous wreck. I couldn't live like that; I won't live like that; so I left."

In response Tonya says, "You say *problem*, does the mean he has only one problem?" When Lacy says that she doesn't mean that, Tonya asks her to explain exactly what she does mean.

Lacy tells her, "I need to know that Luther will come home consistently; that he will call when he is going to be delayed, and that he won't always be so defensive when I inquire concerning his whereabouts. I need to know that he has no reason to keep secrets from me, and that he feels the same way I do about not keeping secrets. I need to know that he won't hide where he goes when he does not come home directly after work, and I need him to consider it a wife's right to know where her husband is at all times. I need him to willingly share this information with me.

"That's asking a lot of a man who is as resistant to revealing his whereabouts as you've indicated he is. But if he is sincere as you say he is, and I have no reason to doubt his sincerity at this point, and if he's willing to be truthful during our sessions together, I'm optimistic. Now Lacy, you *are* aware that it will take Luther's recognition of his problems, and *his* willingness to work toward solving them for the two of you to resolve this situation and get back together?" Tonya asks.

On the way home following the first session, Luther says, "Do you really think that did us any good? As far as I can see, all we did was leave some of our hard-earned money behind and put our business in the street."

"Luther, our business in already *in the street*. Don't you know people already know we're not living together anymore?" she asks. "I had not expected our problems to be solved in just one session. It's going to take time for us to see any results, and that will happen only if you are less resistant and more cooperative," she tells him. Luther says nothing.

Six sessions later, Luther finally admits that *his dad came home, or did not come home, as it pleased him.* "And my mom didn't make any big deal over it. Dad always took care of us; we loved him and we knew he loved us. What more can you expect of a man?" he asks.

The counselor leads Luther so see, for the first time, that he doesn't know whether his mom *made a big deal of it or not, that maybe she just kept her feelings about it hidden from her children.* Now Luther begins to recall the long silences he observed between his parents. As a boy he often wondered why they didn't talk to one another, but had eventually concluded that this was *just normal behavior between parents*. She further leads him to see that even if what he says were true, that doesn't mean that Lacy is going to be accepting of that kind of behavior. She then asks, "How do you think you'd feel and react if the tables were turned, if it were Lacy who didn't come home, didn't call when she didn't come home, and made it clear that she resented it when you questioned her about it?" Tonya tells him not to answer the questions, but to think long and hard about the answers to them.

Following fourteen months of separation, Lacy has agreed to move back home, on a trial basis. "Just weekends at first," Tonya suggests, "and if it works out, then you can make a decision."

That first weekend, they had such a great time reminiscing about high school days, their honeymoon in Hawaii, the early days of their marriage. They felt as if they were on a second honeymoon. Neither of them left the apartment the whole weekend, and had no desire to do so.

They spent weekends together for the next three months. During this period, they continued their counseling sessions. Luther is no longer resistant to the sessions. *He now understands that behaviors which he observed in his father impacted him in a way that he was unaware of.* He now accepts that it isn't fair to expect his wife to accept extended periods of absences with no word from him. He knows that his mother could not have been happy with his father's long periods of absences, nor with the long silences between his parents, which he now attributes to *his missing* father. He's even asked his mother how she felt about that.

Now that his wife has returned to their home and their marriage, he is careful that he doesn't lose her again by perpetuating *the yield* that was his father's deceptive legacy to him.

Chapter XVI
Matthew, Mable, and Discontent

Matthew continues to withdraw; Mable continues to try to get him to open up and share with her what's on his mind. But he insists there's nothing on his mind, that he has no idea why she believes there is something he's withholding from her.

Following months of unease and discontent, Mable makes an appointment to talk with the pastor of their church. When they meet, she talks with him about her and Matt's situation telling him, "
"I have to talk with someone. I just can't talk to him anymore. Whenever I try, he insists there's nothing wrong. But I know Matt. I've been married to this man over several decades. There's no way he'd act as he's been acting for months now if there was not something going on. She relates everything that she feels she can share without violating her husband's privacy.

The pastor tells her that her situation is not at all unusual, that many couples who have been married for a long time have experienced similar problems. He advises her to be understanding and patient, and to pray, that Matt obviously loves her, that the marriage would not have endured harmoniously for almost forty years if that were not so.

Mable feels only slightly better after her conversation with Reverend Henderson. In fact, as she drives home, *she is thinking that maybe she should not have said anything to him about their affairs. He didn't really tell me anything I didn't already know*, she says to her self, *and now he knows more about us than I really want him to know.* This is on her mind as she makes the right turn onto their street.

When she arrives home, Matt is there in his favorite easy chair, an old recliner that has seen better days. She calls, "Hello," as she lets herself in through the kitchen door, which is entered from the garage. Matt does not respond; this is unusual. Mable calls again, "Hello. What time did you get home?" When there is still no response, she walks into the family room, just off the kitchen. Matt's eyes are closed; she believes him to be dozing. She goes to him and shakes him lightly, not wanting to startle him. She says, "Why don't you get into bed for your nap? You'll be more comfortable."

When Matt does not respond, she shakes him less gently. But there is still no response. Matt has suffered a massive heart attack. *He is dead.*

Mable calls both Mamie and Matt, Jr. They are both shaken. Matt was always so healthy and robust. It is hard for them too, but they both try to console their mother; she is inconsolable. Her grief is shattering. *All she can think about is that this could have been the reason why he had been behaving so unlike himself.* She can't believe that the man whom she has

Book II - Yield

loved for most of her life is gone, that she'll never see his smile again; never hear his voice again.

Both Mamie and Matt, Jr. continue to try to console her as best they can, but it isn't consolation she desires, it's Matt, and she knows that's a futile desire, *but she has it nonetheless.* She has cried so much that she is silent at the funeral, grief-striken. She realizes now that for him she will never know what *the yield* was.

Tisha, Tomas, and Yvonne

Tisha misses Tomas so much, but she is angry, bitter about the affair he had with Yvonne. She says to Mae, a close friend of hers, "If he had to cheat on me, why'd he have to do it within my family? There're millions of women out there; he could've picked someone else."

In response Mae says, "Because Yvonne was convenient, and she was willing. It could've been anybody, but she was there, and she was amenable."

"But it wasn't *anybody*. It was Yvonne, and I loved her like a sister. She's the mother of my niece and nephews; my parents love her like a daughter; my brother loves her. So not only do I resent the affair, I resent the violation of my family." Tisha says this heatedly.

Meanwhile, Yvonne is confronted by Brad. "What kind of woman could do what you did? Don't you have any sense of family? Don't you have any morals?" he asks, voice dripping with revulsion.

Yvonne retorts hotly, "Don't you dare lecture me about morals! You're no model of decorum yourself. Don't think I'm stupid! I know what you've been up to!"

"I'm no saint, and I'm not claiming to be," Brad acknowledges. "But I can certainly claim that I haven't violated your family. I can claim that I'd never do anything to belittle you in your family's eyes! How do you expect my parents to be able to include you and me and our kids in family gatherings now? Tell me that?" he asks angrily.

Book II - Yield

Teal

Now Yvonne is quiet. She is *thinking about what he just said.* She really doesn't have the sense of family that Brad has. One of the reasons she married him is because of the warm, lovingly close family which he has.

Yvonne wasn't raised in a closeknit family. For the most part, *she raised herself,* even though she grew up living with her mother. No one has ever talked to her before about *a sense of family or morals or family inclusion.* She feels badly about what she has done. She doesn't want to lose Brad; she doesn't want to lose his family either. She's always felt that she was part of the family, like she belonged. They'd all treated her more than decent; they'd treated her like family. She wouldn't deny that. *Now they won't like me, won't want me anymore,* she says to herself.

Tomas and Tisha's divorce became final about six weeks ago. Terrence's birthday is today. Tisha has planned a party for him at a local McDonald's. Even though she would have preferred not to, she has invited Tomas to the party. Terrence has been so excited about the party. He keeps asking, "Is my dad coming to the party? Will Dad be at my party?" So she relented and called. She left a message with his answering service, glad that he wasn't there and that she didn't have to speak with him; she assumes he got it.

The party is in progress; Tomas is late arriving. Terrence keeps watching the door and looking out the window near where he's seated. *He is hoping to see his dad come through the door.* And he is not disappointed. When Terrence sees Tomas come through the door, his whole countenance lights up, he jumps up and rushes to meet him; he hurls himself at his dad. Tomas grabs him up in a bear hug, swings him high in the air and says, "How's my birthday boy?" Terrence squeals with delight.

Book II - Yield

Teal

Tisha watches all of this without comment. She is thinking, *he could've helped me plan this for him. We could've done it together. He could have been part of his son's daily life, but this is how he wants it.* But this is not the way Tomas wants it. This is just the way it is.

As the party breaks up Tomas says to Tisha, "Can I take you and the boy somewhere for our own private celebration?"

"Like where?" she asks.

"How about to that park where we used to take him all the time? He can play; we can watch him and talk. I *really* miss the two of you," he says. And he does miss the two of them. He had not meant for his liaisons to separate him from his wife and son. He wanted, and had meant for them to be a permanent part of his life. In fact, he'd never even thought of the two of them in relation to *this other part of his life. In his mind they were separate entities, one just for play and fun; the other for substance and commitment.*

Tomas, like too many other Black men, is somehow able to compartmentalize mentally. They are able to tuck their homes and families into one neat little compartment labeled *mine*, and seal off that compartment until it suits them to remove the seal. They are able to put their infidelities, their flings, their one-night stands while they're away on from home, into another neat little compartment and seal it off until another opportune moment occurs. In a third neat little compartment, they are obviously able to seal off thoughts that would force them to recognize and deal with, if only mentally, facts like possible exposure to AIDS, herpes, syphilis, gonorrhea, and a host of other sexually transmitted diseases that many of us have never even heard of that are lurking and ready to pounce upon the unsuspecting. In still another little compartment, they are able to seal off thoughts of exposing their unsuspecting wives to whatever it is to which they expose themselves.

"It's a little late for that, don't you think?" Tisha says in response to Tomas's statement, *I really miss the two of you.*

"It doesn't have to be, you know. People make mistakes, Tisha; people learn from them. I made a mistake. I can admit that. I'm sorry, sorrier than you'll ever know, but I can't undo it. I would if I could; I would in a heartbeat. But I can't. I have learned from it though," he says. Tisha does not make a verbal response, but she is thinking: *it's not undoable, and even if it were, the broken trust is not regainable.*

On the way to the park, Terrence is delighted. He is so happy to have his parents *back together*. He does not understand that they are not back together. All he knows is that they're taking him to his favorite park like they did when his dad lived with them. "Dad, are you coming home to live with us now?" he asks.

"You'll have to talk to your mom about that, Son," Tomas says. Terrence looks over at his mom and then back at his dad. He doesn't know what to say, but somehow he knows that this is not something to ask his mom right now. He looks again at the two of them; *he wonders what is happening.*

"Oh no, don't you tell him that, Tomas. Don't make him believe it's my fault that we're not all living together as a family!" Tisha says passionately. This time Tomas remains silent, but he says to himself: *it is your fault. If you'd allow it, we **would be** living together as a family. I'm not saying that what I did was right, but it doesn't have to separate our family.*

Tomas waits until they arrive at the park and Terrence heads for his favorite slide, then he says to Tisha, "Well, isn't it? "I'm not saying that you don't have good reason for doing what you did; for feeling what you feel, but I am saying we could've worked it out. We didn't have to split. That *was* your decision!" he says this angrily, as if he has given it a lot of thought and has drawn a logical conclusion.

Astounded by his attitude, Tisha says, "Obviously, you think adultery is no big deal. You evidently think it's okay to sleep with any woman in your family who is amenable. Well, I hate to be the one to break it to you, Tomas, but there are some people who feel very strongly about things like *adultery* and *incest*!"

"You hold it! Now I know that what I did is adultery, but I'm not admitting to any incest." Tomas says this heatedly. Tisha, however, does not back down.

"You know what, Tomas? It's our thinking, that's where you and I part company. To me, *family is family*. My blood doesn't have to be running through someone's veins for me to consider him or her family. Your brothers are my family too. I'd never sleep with either of them, even now. I can see how divergent our thinking is, and therein lies our dilemma." Tisha says this quietly, but drives her point home more thoroughly than if she'd shouted it.

Tomas has no rebuttal. He realizes that what she says is entirely true. *Not once has he thought of Yvonne as family*; if he had, he would not have slept with her. But he does think of Tisha and Terrence as his family, even now, and he isn't happy living apart from them. He's never lacked for female companionship, before or since he and Tisha separated, but there's no satisfaction, no contentment in his life now. That's what he longs for most.

Book II - Yield

Teal

After several moments of silence he says to Tisha, "What do I have to do to get you back? *I need you; I need my son.* I want to see the two of you everyday. I want to share in your lives. Tisha, I love you; I love our son. What can I say to make you understand?"

"I'll never understand how you could do what you did; it's incomprehensible, Tomas. I believe you love Terrence; you may even love me, but your love for us didn't *stay your hand*. It wasn't the motivating force nor the deterrent that it should have been. I'm sorry, but I don't want you back. Our son needs stability; he needs good role models to emulate. I need a husband whom I can trust, someone that I don't have to keep tabs on, even when we're at family gatherings. You don't offer either of these."

Tomas is sorry too, but *the yield* became his medium of exchange. He traded his family for it.

Book II - Yield

Nikki, Shree, and Mike

Nikki's baby, a boy whom she named Charles, was born a month ago. Mike never called her again after he started dating Shree, so she *never* told him about the pregnancy. Her feelings she expressed to her friend, Jacky, when she told her, "If he doesn't want me, I don't want him. If he is capable of dating me exclusively for half a year, at least I thought it was exclusive; I know I wasn't dating anyone else, and then disappearing without so much as by-your-leave, then I'm, we're, better off without him."

Shree decides to have an abortion. As a junior in college, Shree knew that she wasn't ready for a child. When she tells Mike that she is pregnant, he encourages her to have the abortion. "You're too young and beautiful to be saddled with a baby. There's plenty of time for babies, after you've graduated and lived a little. Let me know how much it'll cost and I'll get the money to you," he says.

"That won't be necessary. I have my own money, which my grandparents left to me, so I won't even have to tell my parents about this. I don't want them to know," Shree tells him.

Mike is relieved. He knows her parents slightly through the company where he works, so it could've been messy if Shree had chosen a different course, but he doesn't have to worry about that now.

Shree returns to college more than a week early to have the abortion. She wants to allow for some recuperative time, *if she needs it*, and she doesn't want that to happen in her parents' home. She knows how concerned they are for her and how much they love her, and she wants to spare them the stress of this situation. As their only child, they have always been overprotective, and she accepts this as one of the ways they demonstrate their love for her. She loves them dearly too. She expects to hear from Mike, anticipating that he will be concerned about how everything turns out. *But Mike does not call.* Several months have now passed since the abortion and Shree has accepted that Mike *isn't going to call,* that his chief concern was her body; that he has no interest in her now.

Time has a way of creeping past while no one is watching, and so Charles is now a boy of seven. He is a beautiful and intelligent boy. Nikki has been a wonderful mother and she loves him deeply; he loves her too. He has been begging her for several months now to let him play baseball in one of the pee wee leagues. Every summer when he visits with his grandparents, his grandfather shows him his old, treasured black and white films of the Black Baseball League in which he once played. The two of them spend hours watching and rewatching these silent films, for which Grandpop Riley provides the commentary. Charles has loved the game for as long as he can remember knowing of its existence.

Nikki has registered him this season to play in one of these leagues. Because of her job responsibilities, she has arranged for him to ride to his practices with a neighbor of theirs who has a son playing in the same league, on the same team. But she plans to be there herself for the final segments of the practice sessions, and to drive him and the neighbor's son home afterwards.

As Nikki parks the car and heads for the bleachers, she recognizes Mike as the coach. Except for a slightly receding hairline, he looks the same. Mike's company encourages its employees to get involved in the community. Mike began coaching the team as a result of this encourangement, but was

Book II - Yield

Teal

pleasantly surprised to find that he enjoys it. This is his fourth year of coaching, and to his astonishment, he finds that he takes pleasure in his interactions with the kids, frequently arranging to take them to McDonalds after some of the games in order to extend the time that he spends with them, as well as to indulge them.

He encountered a bout with mumps about five years ago, so Mike knows that he will never be able to father a child. For the most part, this does not bother him. In fact, when he first learned that he was sterile, he was glad, though he decided to share this information with no one, fearing that it might *damage his image.*

Nikki knows none of this as she sees Mike for the first time in almost eight years. But she does know that Mike is a *big man* now. From time to time she has read about his accomplishments in the local news, and has seen him speak on local television broadcasts. She also knows that *she does not want Charles to know that Mike is his father; she does not want Mike to know that Charles is his son.*

Several days later as Mike examines the team roster, he sees the name Charles Smaw. He recalls a woman whom he dated several years ago with that same last name. He wonders *if they are related. Momentarily he reminisces about the period when he dated Nikki.* From time to time throughout the past seven years, Mike has thought about her and has *wondered what happened to her.* He knows that he treated her shabbily, that he should have called and broken it off, but that wasn't his style back then. His was a *love 'em and leave 'em* style. Breaking if off usually meant explanations, tears; stress. He didn't like confrontations, so when he lost interest, when he no longer wanted a woman in his life, *he just stopped calling her.*

"That Smaw kid is *good!*" says one of the assistant coaches to Mike several weeks into the season. The team is playing their third game and Charles is pitching. "He's had a homerun just about every game, and he can pitch too; has a lot of speed on that ball for one so young. Look how he pitches. Have you met his parents? Are they here today?"

Following the game, the coaches take the team to McDonalds. As they are waiting for their orders, Mike moves over to position himself near where Charles is standing in line awaiting his food order. "Charles, do your parents come to the games?" he asks. Charles says that his mom comes to all the games. "What's your mom's name? I think I know your mother," he says. Charles tells him that his mom's name is Nikki. "I once dated a woman named Nikki Smaw," Mike says. "I believe your mother may be that woman."

"No kidding. Awesome!" Charles says as he reaches for his order, and stuffs a fry in his mouth.

Later that night as Charles is getting ready for bed he relates the conversation he had with his coach to his mom. "Is that right?" is the only response she makes. But she is wondering *if she can come up with an excuse Charles will accept to get him off the team. She's not getting good vibes about this situation. She feels apprehensive; her stomach flutters nervously.*

Meanwhile, Mike has been thinking, *wondering when it was that he dated Nikki; wondering also if Charles could be his son. I wouldn't mind having a son like that,* he mentally acknowledges. *The next time Nikki comes to a game, I'm going to have a talk with her.* He's thinking about this as he showers and readies himself for bed.

When Charles and Nikki leave the next two games before Mike can untangle himself from some of the other players and parents, he decides to call her at home. He looks at the team roster which lists players' names, addresses, and telephone numbers. Charles answers the phone on the first ring. He's acquired the habit now of rushing to get it before Nikki does. "Mom, it's for you," he yells. "I think it's my coach," he whispers.

Nikki *does not want* to talk to Mike, and she does not know exactly why, but she feels afraid. She takes the phone only because she does not know how to avoid it. Charles has huge eyes glued to her, waiting intently for her to say something. "Hello, what can I do for you?" she says.

"Good evening," Mike says cordially. "I was wondering if I could come over and take you and Charles out to dinner one evening this week? I tried to catch the two of you before you left the game today, but you got away before I could get untangled. I once dated a woman with your exact name, and I was wondering if you're that same woman," he tells her.

"Charles and I are very busy. I'm sorry, but we won't be able to go out with you. And yes, I'm that woman. We did go out for a while, but that was a *long* time ago."

But Mike is persistent. He's been doing a lot of thinking about Charles and Nikki. He's realized that if Nikki had been married to Charles' father, neither of them would be using Nikki's maiden name of Smaw, probably. He's recognized that he could already have a beautiful and talented son, even though he is now unable to father a child. He has *no intention* of failing to pursue this. *In my position, I could probably get custody; if not total, joint perhaps,* he says to himself. "Nikki," he says, "if not dinner, can I come over and just talk?"

"I'm sorry, but we're very busy," she says. Mike does not push at this point, but he feels sure that Nikki has something which she wants kept from him. *Women don't usually say no to him, so why is Nikki so insistent that she and Charles are busy?* he asks himself.

"I'm sorry to hear that," he says. "Some other time then." These words trigger an instant flashback for Nikki. With unexpected clarity she instantly recalls that phone conversation, almost a decade ago, when she waited until the last minute to call Mike to cancel the date she had with him to attend his company's annual picnic. She was hoping he wouldn't want to go to the picnic without her. She was hoping he'd say that he would come over to her place and take care of her. But what he said was, "I'm sorry to hear that." As she hangs up the phone, she says to herself, *same old Mike. Not only do some things never change; some people never change either.*

As soon as Nikki hangs up the phone, Charles wants to know, "Was that my coach? What did he want? Does he want to date you again? Are you going out with him?"

"Questions, questions," Nikki says. "It's bedtime for you, young man." She hugs and kisses him good night. He wipes off the kiss, feigning a repulsive *yuk!* They share the warmth and laughter of a beloved parent and child as she tucks him in.

While lying in bed, Mike is wondering how he can find out more about Charles. Mike has friends in high places. He shouldn't have too much trouble learning what he wants to know. He gets up and makes a phone call. Harris, his friend who works in the statistics office downtown at the courthouse tells him that he'll see what he can find out and will get back to him tomorrow. Then Harris asks, "Why're you so interested in this kid?" Charles is vague, saying something about needing exact dates of births of his ballplayers to assure their qualifications for the pee wee baseball league in which he coaches.

The following week Mike arranges to catch Nikki and Charles as they are getting ready to leave the ballpark. Nikki is unlocking her car; Charles is standing at the door opposite the driver's side. He says to the two of them, "If you guys haven't eaten dinner yet, let me join you. My treat."

Before Nikki has a chance to respond, Charles says, "Can we, Mom, can we?" He sounds so eager, Nikki doesn't have the heart to say no. Instead, she says, "Charles still has homework to do; we should get on home."

"You guys go on home so Charles can get started on that homework. I'll order *takeou*t and bring it over. What'll you say, Nikki? Charles?" He looks pleadingly from one to the other. Charles' eyes are as big as saucers as he watches the two of them.

Nikki doesn't feel that she can say *no* to this offer gracefully. She reluctantly assents. It's obvious to her that Charles wants her to accept the offer. His eyes glow at the prospect of having dinner with his coach.

Dinner and homework are complete; Charles is in bed asleep. Both Nikki and Mike have made light, polite conversation while eating and while putting the leftover food into the refrigeratior. Now Nikki says, "Why this sudden interest, Mike? What is this all about?"

Mike does not hedge. "I know about the boy, Nikki. It's wrong; it isn't fair the way you kept it from me. I had a right to know; I have a right to know, a right to be a part of his life. He's my son."

Nikki is angered by these comments. "When was I supposed to let you know, Mike, during one of your many phone calls after I found out he was on the way?" she asks sarcastically. "Or maybe I should've told you when you came by to see how I was feeling right after the picnic."

Mike had forgotten all about that long ago picnic, but he now remembers it clearly, as though this all happened a few weeks ago as opposed to nearly a generation. He immediately thinks: *I'll bet that's when she first knew she was pregnant with him. Fleetingly, he recalls Shree, and that for a brief time, she too carried his child.*

Mike can see that he has upset her. This is not what he wants to do. He says, "That was shabby of me, Nikki, I know that. But I was young and cocky, and I didn't understand what was important."

"And you do now, " she says.

"I do now," he responds.

They look deeply into one another's eyes for a long time; both are silent. Nikki is *thinking about that long ago time when she felt so sick in her body, and so wounded in her spirit*. Mike is thinking *that he could've helped shape not just the physical characteristics, but the character of that beautiful boy asleep upstairs. He could've presented his parents with that much-wanted grandchild to which they frequently allude whenever he visits them.* Finally, Mike says, "Give me a chance to get to know him, Nikki. I really want this."

"Mike, I know this is going to be difficult to assimilate, but life isn't about what Mike *really* wants. Can you handle that?"

"Okay, I probably deserve that," Mike admits, "but I want you to know that I'm not the same selfish guy you knew nearly a decade ago. Give me a chance to prove it to you. Let me spend some time with the two of you. Please, think it over. You know the boy needs a father in his life. I *am* and want to be *his father*. Give what I've said some serious thought. I'm going now, but you'll be hearing from me," he says as he walks toward the door.

Nikki toys with the idea of telling Mike that Charles isn't his son, but Nikki is basically an honest woman, and lying goes against her grain. *Besides*, she says to herself, *with all of the DNA and other testing possible today, he'd probably find out anyhow. The last thing I want to do is disrupt Charles' life, threaten his happiness; his peace of mind. Perhaps if I behave amicably, talk to him, maybe go out with him a few times, he'll just go away.*

Mike begins to call Nikki almost daily. He wants to know if he can stop by, or if she and Charles would like to go out to breakfast on Saturday, or maybe to Sunday Brunch, or how about dinner tonight? Sometimes he says he has tickets for this baseball game, or a show that all the kids are raving about and would love to take the two of them.

Summer is approaching. Mike wants to know if Charles can attend a baseball camp that comes highly recommended for kids his age. "He's *really* good," Mike tells Nikki. "He pitches like a little pro. That kid's got *some* arm on him. I'd like him to have the experience of that camp. Let him go Nikki. It'll be my pleasure to pay for it. I'll even drive him there, if you'll allow it," he hastens to add.

"I don't think so," Nikki says. "Good-bye, Mike."

Mike's frustration is escalating. He is used to getting what he wants. *And now he wants his son; he wants to be a part of his son's life. He wants to see him everyday; he wants to make plans for Charles. He wants to throw balls to him in a backyard which has been equipped by him especially for his son. He wants to stand in the ballpark and proudly point to Charles as **his** son. He wants Charles to spend part, if not all, of his summers with **him**. He wants to show him off to his family. He wants the decision to send Charles to baseball camp to be **his** to make. He determines to do what he can to see that each of these wants becomes a reality.*

One of Mike's closest friends, Cullen, is a lawyer. He is thinking that *perhaps he should call Cullen and ask him what the possibilities are.* That weekend he and Cullen meet at a local athletic club for a few games of squash. As the two of them leave the courts and head for the showers Mike says, "Hypothetically, if a man has a kid, one that he didn't know about for, say six or seven years, and then he learns of the child, does the man have any rights as a father?"

In response Cullen says, "Hypothetically, does this man know for certain that this is his child, and exactly what rights does this father want, hypothetically?"

Meanwhile, Nikki has met a man, a wonderful man, who has swept her off her feet. Barkley has his own business, a small but thriving computer firm. He has met Charles and they really hit it off. He has taken the two of them out to dinner and to the movies several times. He has spent the night in their home, though Nikki insisted he leave long before Charles awakened on those mornings. *Barkley and Nikki are in love, head over hills in love.*

Barkley wants her for his wife, and he doesn't want to wait! Nikki wants to be his wife. *Why not?* she asks herself. *He likes Charles, and Charles likes him, and I know he'll be good for Charles. I'm gonna do it!* she suddenly decides.

Charles has been with his grandparents now for almost a month. Nikki and Barkley have flown to Las Vegas for the weekend. They were married two hours ago. They are radiantly happy, intoxicated with each other. Barkley is saying to her, "You know I travel a lot; I have to, and I want you and Charles with me whenever Charles isn't in school. I don't want you tied to a job that'll keep that from happening. Would you mind giving up your job?"

"Barkley," she says, "I don't want to think of anything mundane just now. I'm too happy to think of anything but this." And she gives him a passionate, lingering kiss. He too loses his interest in the mundane; his thinking capacity is seriously diminished just then.

Barkley wants to adopt Charles. He wants Charles to have his name. He and Nikki discuss the pros and cons of this. They talk to Charles about it; he likes the idea. Proceedings are begun.

When Mike learns of this, he is furious. *She can't do this!* he tells himself. *She can't just give my son away to another man like I have no say-so in the matter.* But the truth of the matter is, he has no say-so in the matter. When he could have had his way as well as his say, he chose to remain silent. Now the only child that he will ever have is lost to him as a direct consequence of his quest for *the yield.*

Chapter XVII

Stewart Stealing

Following Stewart's arrest, Greta goes down to the police station to see if she can straighten things out. *She's certain there's been some grave error.* She absolutely cannot imagine he'd do anything illegal. She knows that he loves her; she knows that he loves their children. She tells herself that *he'd never do anything to jeopardize the family; that is as important to him as it is to her.* But still, *she is afraid.* They've never been involved with the law before. Greta's not exactly sure what she needs to do; to whom she needs to speak.

At the police station she goes up to the desk sergeant and says, "My husband was brought here less than an hour ago. I'm sure there's been a mistake. I'd like to see him. May I?" The sergeant tells her that her husband is being processed and will not be allowed visitors until that procedure is completed, if then. She says, "Who can I see about having him released? I'm sure there's been a big mistake, maybe even a case of mistaken identity."

"Ma'am, if you had any idea how many times I've heard that statement, and of how few times I've found it to be accurate, you'd probably have said something more original. What is you husband's name?" he asks.

She gives him the name; he gets up and goes through a door marked, *Private*. Greta sits and ponders; she feels terrible. She has left the children alone at home. She is thinking that *maybe she should call Marge, their neighbor, and ask her to go over and check on the kids*. As she is thinking this, the sergeant comes back through the door.

Sergeant Chase tells her that she can see her husband now, but for only a short time. He leads her to a small, dingy room where Stewart is being held. She looks at him a long time before speaking, hoping that through some muted, osmotic process she is able to discern his thoughts. As she stares at him, a great suffocating surge of anxiety engulfs her. She knows this man; she loves this man. He has been her husband for more than a decade. Suddenly she recognizes that if this were some egregious error, he would not be standing here silently; meekly.

Finally, Greta says, "Stewart, tell me about it." He remains silent for a few seconds longer, eyes on the floor, thoughts arching. When he looks up, his eyes glisten with tears.

"Oh, Greta, I don't even know how to begin. I can't believe I allowed myself to get involved in this."

"Tell me exactly what *this* is," she says.

Stewart explains to Greta about being approached by Joe and Carl, whom she knows from the annual company picnics. "I know nothing about what took place during the past several years, which is what the investigation is focusing upon. I've been involved for the past three months only, and the only unlawful thing I've done is to help load rolls of carpet onto a truck that doesn't belong to the company. I know that what I did was wrong. I know I should have just told them to get lost; that I wasn't interested when they approached me, but I was thinking about all we could do with that extra money. It seemed so harmless; so easy, and they'd gotten away with it for years," he concludes.

"Did you think about the kids and me? Did it occur to you what something like this would do to our family?" she asks.

He doesn't say so, but he didn't. Not once did he consider what being caught, being arrested as part of a theft ring, would do to his family. They were given no consideration, even though it is their lives that will be inevitably altered by his decision.

Stewart, like far too many other Black men who are currently incarcerated, makes potentially life-altering, frequently life shattering decisions without considering the family first. It is obvious that scores of Black men are not cognizant of the fact that every decision they make that has the potential to impact their families in a negative manner, should be made with the family foremost in mind. Possible repercussions upon the family ought to be the determining factor. When a married man makes a decision without considering its possible impact upon his family, he is saying, nonverbally, that he prefers *the yield* to the family.

Lauren, Luis, and Dr. Pat

Lauren's lawyer advises her not to sign anything presented to her by Luis for her signature. "Read everything carefully, especially all fine print, and let me see it if there is any question about its clarity." Penelope reminds her that she and the children are accustomed to a certain standard of living and that if it can be maintained, then it should be. She also tells her, "The children's educational funds must be maintained, and I suggest Luis's name be removed from that. I'll speak with his representative and get back to you."

As Lauren leaves Penelope's office, she sees Luis mounting the steps of the hospital across the street. She can't stand the sight of him. Every time she sees him, she recalls anew the scene in the hotel room in Seattle where he lay with Dr. Pat in his arms. *How could he do this?* She asks herself for the thousandth time. *How could he put at risk what we've shared with one another? The memories, the struggle, the children, the contentment...? Someone wise once said, "The joy lies in the struggle," and I never believed that, but maybe it's true for some people,* she says to herself. *Maybe Luis no longer felt as I felt, as I know he once felt.* Lauren keeps thinking about it; she can't shut it out, not even to sleep, it seems.

Lauren is bitter, *very bitter*. She trusted Luis implicitly. Never, once did she suspect that he would be unfaithful to her. Even now, nearly two years later, the pain of betrayal is as raw as it was the day the wound was inflicted. For months after she learned of it, she was immobilized, so stunned by the fact, the revelation of it. Now, she is suing Luis for divorce.

She is asking for total custody of the children, and for her fair share of the medical practice, in cash.

Luis, however, does not have the cash; in fact, he is still paying off medical school loans as well as the loan that he and Lauren secured when he purchased his share of the practice. He has tried to reason with Lauren, but Lauren is in no mood to be reasoned with, nor has she been since all of this started. During their latest conversation when he pleaded with her to be reasonable, she questioned, "Why should you expect me to be what you obviously aren't?" When he asked what she meant by that, she retorted, "How reasonable was it to begin an affair with a coworker? No! Forget the *coworker* part. How reasonable was it to begin an affair, period, when you knew you were a married man with a family you claim to love; children who adore you, a wife who loved and trusted you; a life we all sacrificed to build?" With no adequate response, Luis remains silent.

Invisible but dominating, the anger lingers. It colors everything. She finds herself screaming at the children for some minor infraction one or the other has committed. After all this time, she still finds it hard, and sometimes impossible, to fall asleep at night. She knows that she needs professional help, but she doesn't want it; she isn't ready to release the anger. It's her only link with sanity, and she feels that without it she'll break down completely. Whenever she feels the hysteria or mounting, all she has to do is recall the anger and for a brief period it gets her past the madness.

Luis is feeling the pressure, increasingly. He wants Lauren to agree *to put their house on the market, to move into a less expensive place.* "No way, Buddy!" she tells him. We were doing fine. We were having no problems meeting our obligations. You broke it; *you* fix it! You made me part of the problem, I will not voluntarily be a part of the solution to a problem you created all by yourself! I'm not moving my children, further disrupting their lives by altering their environment. They've had enough traumatic disruptions in their young lives. So you do whatever you have to do, but we're staying right here!" she says as she gets up and walks out.

For the first time ever, Luis calls in sick. He doesn't make his rounds at the hospital. The stress is getting to him. He really is sick: *soul sick; spirit sick; life sick.* Earl and Stanley are concerned; they agree to cover for him. Dr. Pat calls, wanting to know why he didn't come in and how he is doing. He tells her that he is okay, but he feels awkward around her now, talking to her even feels awkward. He knows that this is a foolish and childish way to feel, but *he feels as though she is responsible for his predicament.* Though he did ask her out a few times after Lauren and he separated, he avoids her as much as possible now. He arrives at the clinic only minutes before his first scheduled appointment, unless there is a meeting scheduled or he has to take care of some other business there; he leaves as soon as he sees his final patient at the clinic for the day. He also tries to avoid Earl and Stanley. *He feels uneasy around them too, as if they are omniscient observers who are privy to all that has happened and is happening in his private life, and that they are silently disapproving.*

He misses his children, especially Lisa. He misses her even when they are together. She's not the same precocious, loquacious, uninhibited child with whom he loved interacting. She's more subdued now, quieter; more introspective. He misses having Laurence meet him at the door and leap into his arms as if he's been gone for weeks rather than a few hours. He misses having Lauren in his arms in bed, or feeling her perfect fit as she adjusts herself into his hunker like a warm, cosseted, familiar blanket. He realizes just how much it cost him to finance *the yield*.

Megan, Randy, and Gretel

Something tells Megan that Gretel is pregnant. She isn't showing, but Megan gets this instantaneous, clear, intuitive vision and immediately the thought occurs to her: *this woman is carrying Randy's child.* She looks from Randy to Gretel, feeling an overwhelming impulse to reach out and slap them simultaneouly. But the hurt overrides the anger. *How can a man get married of his own choosing, one month, and move in with another woman the next month?* she asks herself. *I've heard so many women say that some men are dogs, pigs even, but I never wanted to believe that; I never did believe it! It isn't even human to behave like that. Now I don't know what to think. Some animals even mate for life!* All of this passes through Megan's mind as she stands there looking at Randy. She turns and bolts from the house.

Randy says to Gretel, "I have to go after her." *And he does.* He follows Megan, running, calling her name as he runs. Megan sees a taxi and hails it;. she rushes and gets in before Randy can catch up to her. She says to the driver, "Go, just go," gesturing to assure that the driver understands that she wants him to drive away immediately.

Randy stands there looking after the taxi. *She shouldn't have come here like this,* he says to himself; *he wonders where she is going; he wonders how she got all the way to Germany, and why she didn't let him know she was coming. She shouldn't have come here like this. This is all her fault,* he actually believes right at that moment. He goes to the barracks where he used to live and uses the phone book there to list the phone numbers of area hotels.

It doesn't take long to find the one where Megan is registered. It is he this time who hails the taxi. When he arrives at the hotel, he can see Megan sitting on a stool at the bar; he goes into the crowded bar and stands beside her. He tries to take her hand, but she snatches it away. He tries to think of a plausible lie, but he can't. He asks when she got there and why she hadn't told him that she was coming. She doesn't answer right away, and when she does, she asks quietly, so quietly in fact that he has to strain to hear her, "How was I supposed to do that, Randy? You no longer live in the barracks; that's the only address I have for you. Have you forgotten that?" *He had. He had forgotten that completely!*

"It's too noisy in here. Come on, please. Let's go to your room so that I can explain," Randy says. In the room he tells her that he met Gretel shortly after he arrived in Germany. He tells her that Gretel got pregnant, that he hadn't meant for that to happen, but when it did, he felt some obligation to her.

To this she says, "Did you feel no obligation to me; to the vows we so recently exchanged? Tell me this, Randy: if I hadn't come here, would you ever have told me about this? Would you have lived here with that German woman for two whole years, all the while writing lies to me, feigning uncertainty about your tour of duty, and then have come home to me pretending to have missed me just as much as I'd missed you?" When Randy does not respond, Megan continues. "What could you have been thinking about, Randy, having unprotected sex with someone you hardly know? What are you using for brains?"

Randy continues to remain silent, but he has begun to *think about the fact that he did not know Gretel when he first had sex with her; that he hardly knows her now.* He can't speak German, and Gretel can't speak English, though they've both learned a few words of each. He feels a little frightened now. *What if she does have something?* he asks himself for the first time. Now he says, "I didn't think. All I could think of was missing you and needing you. She was just a substitute for you. You must know that! It was you I wanted."

"I wanted you too after you left, but I didn't find some willing substitute and move in with him, or allow him to move in with me. I expected better from you, Randy. I deserve better. I thought your love meant what mine meant: fidelity, trust; loyalty. I can *never* trust you now, surely you understand that. You've got almost two years left over here. You'd been unfaithful to me before you'd been here for two weeks, so I'd never be able to believe, no matter what you said or did, that you spent the remaining months of your tour practicing abstinence."

"You can trust me. I'll never do anything like this again; I swear," he says pleadingly.

"You can't undo it this time. That baby she's carrying is a fact of life, a life you irresponsibly helped to create. Do *one* responsible thing in all this. You'll be obligated to that child for at least eighteen years. Be man enough to treat somebody right!"

Randy tells her that this is not what he wants, that he loves her and he wants their marriage to continue. *But it is not to be.* She says, "Fidelity is not an optional ingredient within a marriage, Randy, not within my marriage. You've got two more years over here, so do what is right by that German woman and the child that she's expecting."

Randy makes no oral response, but he is cognizant that his attraction to *the yield* has cost him his bride.

CHAPTER XVIII

Donna, Neil, and Mannin

Donna's sons, Donald and Dale, Jr. try unsuccessfully to get Donna to tell them what happened between her and Mannin. All she will say is that *things just didn't work out*. But they can see how hurt she is. They can see that she is no longer the happy, youthful mother to whom they are accustomed. Each of them tries to visit her more often, hoping to cheer her, and she does try when they're with her to put their minds at ease, but she hasn't been able to shake the depression. Work does provide a measure of forgetfulness, but at times, even in the midst of a difficult case, she finds her mind drifting, thinking about what happened. *I never should have married him*, she tells herself for the thousandth time. *I should've known better, but for a time we were so happy. I just don't understand*, she thinks repeatedly.

Shortly after the breakup Mannin moved in with Lorraine, the woman who was in the yellow Mustang that morning when Donna drove over to his law firm. But after only three months he moved out, telling himself that he just wasn't happy there. A couple of months later, Shana, an aspiring model whom he met through the work he was doing on one of his cases, moved in with him. It lasted six months. After Shana, there was Sissy, then Cookie. But there has been no contentment in any of these relationships, none of the essential unity he craves.

Donna continues to be approached for dates. She is still a very attractive woman. She always declines. She feels as though *men are jokes, so shallow; so superficial.* She has no respect for men. Neither Dale, nor Neil, nor Mannin turned out to be what either had represented himself as when he was dating her. As she and Joy, her closest friend, are having lunch together this Saturday, they are discussing men. Joy is also recently divorced and does not feel very good about men at the moment, but she isn't bitter, just a bit cynical where men are concerned. Donna says, "They have this unique ability to present themselves as so earnest, so interested, so intelligent. But as soon as you really get to know one, you find out that his brains are not located anywhere in his upper extremities."

In response Joy says, "You know I've had my share of jerk experiences, but I'm just not ready to judge all men by the few lousy ones I've known intimately. I agree that they seem to have a unique chameleon quality, but they don't blend very long. They're like kids: they want the toy, they beg for the toy, but when they get it home, the interest ends when the challenge ends. They hardly play with it, and then only if someone else comes along and shows an interest in it. It's ludicrous!"

They continue their conversation as they leave the restaurant and head for the mall. Pointing to a car in one of the lanes opposite theirs Joy says, "Isn't that Mannin Wexler?"

Donna looks; it is Mannin. He sees her and waves; she ignores him, but Joy waves and says, "He is a hunk, even if he is also a two-timing jerk."

"He is a hunk," Donna retorts, "but a hunk of what, should be the concern of his next bedmate."

"Girl stop!" Joy says as she laughs.

The divorce has been final for almost two years now, and Mannin still has found no one with whom he has been content. He has been with a string of women since he and Donna first separated, but there's been no one with her instinct for elegance, no one with her quiet wit, no one with the undisguised affection for him which he remembers emanating so conspicuously from her eyes. He recalls the seven months of sheer joy he and Donna spent together, and he knows that nothing else in his life has ever come close to that. He perceives that he has intentionally relinquished something precious and rare for *the yield*.

Gina, Alvin, and Infidelity

When Alvin and the girls return from his parents' home later that day, the girls are still excited. They want Gina to see the gifts that *Santa* left for them at Gramma and Papa's. They run into the house bringing a chorus of "Mom, Mom, Mom!" Gina comes out of the kitchen smiling, despite the lump in her throat. *My girls are worth it all,* she thinks fleetingly, as she bends to give each of them a hug. Alvin says hello too, but she doesn't acknowledge it, simulating interest in the girl's gifts.

The girls are in bed asleep. Gina has fed them turkey sandwiches and hot chocolate; she has read them a favorite bedtime story. They are happy; everything is right with their world. As she leaves their room, she is thinking that *she is grateful that they are not cognizant of the turmoil which currently exists between her and Alvin.* All three of them adore Alvin and love him as only children are capable of loving: *blindly.*

She goes into the family room and sits on the sofa. Seconds later, Alvin appears with two glasses of champagne. He sets one on the coffee table in front of her. "Gina, please listen to me," he says. "I know it looks bad, but it is not as it appears." Alvin has been thinking all day about what he will say to her. "Those condoms do not belong to me. You know that Paxton and I sometimes share a room to cut down on expenses when we travel; those are his condoms. I must have inadvertently put them into my shaving kit when I picked up the other items I'd taken out and left on the bathroom counter. I know I've given you no reason to feel that you can believe what I say, but this is the truth whether you believe it or not. They must've fallen out of the shaving kit into the larger bag as we traveled. He had already packed his things, so I just assumed everything left on the counter belonged to me, and I put everything left there in my bag."

Gina wants to believe him, but she knows that she cannot trust Alvin to be truthful, that he will lie if lying suits his purposes. She is torn between her desire to believe him and her knowledge that he has probably just made up the story to appease her. She asks him how they could've fallen out of a zipped up shaving bag. "Remember, Gina, the zipper on that bag is broken now; it doesn't zip. I must've mentioned it to you I mentioned it to mom, in fact, she bought me a new one for Christmas, a really nice one too. That one is almost five years old."

Alvin has deliberately broken the zipper on the small, leather bag. It was only earlier today when he saw what his mother had given him for Christmas that he thought up the story which he has just told her. "Alvin, you know, it's sad when married people can't trust one another. I think it's sad when two people who share three beautiful little girls between them can't just take for granted that anything they say to one another is entirely true. I think it's sad when married people have legitimate reasons for doubting one another. I didn't ask you to marry me, Alvin, you asked me to marry you. What did you think that meant? Did you think we could remain newlyweds forever? Did you think I could remain new and exciting to you forever? Don't you know that the only things that stay new are those things that never get used?"

"Gina," Alvin says, "where is all this coming from? Didn't you hear any of what I've just said?"

"I heard you. I just don't know whether it's the truth or not. I'm also baffled about how you could pick up condoms belonging to someone else, accidentally," she says.

"Think about it, Gina. Don't you think if they were mine, I'd have taken greater care to make sure you didn't see them? It's because they are not mine that I gave no thought to them. How could I? I didn't even know they were there. I just picked up everything left there on that counter; I assumed everything there belonged to me. I paid no attention to what I was putting into my bag."

Gina makes no response to what Alvin has just said. Some of it does make sense, but still she knows that he can't be trusted, and that knowledge is painful to her. She wants to believe him, desperately, for all of their sakes, but she still has her doubts.

Later, as they get ready for bed, she says to him, "Alvin, whose responsibility is it to keep excitement alive within a marriage?" Again Alvin wonders where all of this is coming from; where it is headed. He doesn't like these discussions. They make him uncomfortable.

He hedges, "What do you mean?" he asks.

"The question has no hidden meaning, Alvin. It's a simple question. Exactly what part of it needs clarification?"

He bristles; his voice rises an octave. It always irritates him when Gina gets sarcastic with him. Gina knows this and usually makes an effort to avoid sarcasm, but this time she does not care. "Nobody's. I don't know. Why're you asking something like that?"

"I need to know what you think, Alvin. I think one of the reasons for the problems we're having is that we don't really know what one another thinks about some very important issues. *So let's just talk.*"

Alvin doesn't want to talk; he doesn't feel like talking. He wants to make love to Gina. *He wants to feel that things are okay between them again.* This is what is on his mind as Gina stands there fluffing her pillow in the sexy negligee he got her for Christmas. *But I might as well resign myself to this little chat,* he says to himself.

"It is someone's responsibility, Alvin. Nothing desirable lasts unless someone assumes responsibility for its upkeep, and that goes for excitement within a marriage as well as anything else desirable that either one of us can think of. So I ask you again, whose job would you say it is to keep excitement alive within a marriage?"

Alvin thinks about what she has just asked for a few seconds, then he says, "Why does it have to be anybody's job. Excitement isn't a job; it's something that just happens between a man and his wife when they love each other.

Gina counters with, "That's not entirely true, Alvin, although do I agree that excitement is an automatic component for a long time between married people who love each other. But after years of togetherness, years of childrearing, years of day after day mundane but necessary activities, excitement is not just automatic anymore. But neither is it an optional commodity within a marriage, if the marriage is to survive and thrive. So someone has to assume responsibility for keeping excitement alive. Tell me if I'm wrong, but I think the cheating so many men do, and women too, can be traced to a lack of excitement within their marriages."

Alvin doesn't like all of this talk about excitement, and cheating and necessary, mundane activities, but Gina is still standing, holding her pillow. She doesn't appear anywhere close to dropping this conversation, so Alvin says, "Whose responsibility do you think it is?"

Gina was hoping he'd get around to asking her that. She says, "The responsibility rests with both parties, Alvin. It relieves each person of having to assume total responsibility, but at the same time, it obligates each person. That's as it ought to be. Marriage is a partnership; both partners ought to work at keeping it alive and healthy."

As they get into bed Alvin says, "Come here; I'll show you excitement. But Gina doesn't move toward him.

Instead she says, "I'm not interested in excitement just now, Alvin. *We need to talk.* I want to find out what makes you tick. I thought I knew, but I don't really, do I? I thought we were a lot alike when it comes to things like love and family and intimacy. But that's not true, is it? Tell me what our family means to you, Alvin?"

"Gina, you know I love you; you know I love those babies upstairs. There isn't anything I wouldn't do for you and our girls, and you know that," he answers.

"I do believe you love us," she says. "But I also know that it isn't true that there isn't anything you wouldn't do for us."

"What do you mean by that?" he questions.

"Would you give up other women for us?" Gina asks.

"I don't have any other women to give up. What are you talking about?" he asks. Though he is cognizant.

Gina tells him that she doesn't mean that he has other women for whom he feels responsible, that she means is he willing to be faithful to her for the rest of their lives; that she means is he willing to think seriously about the likelihood that their girls will have to be raised by other people if he has exposed, or does expose her or himself to some life-threatening disease? She tells him that she isn't asking him for answers to these questions, she's just asking him to think, to use his brain before he uses any of his other body parts.

Alvin has lost the urge for sex just now. As he lies there in the dark beside Gina, he is thinking for the first time *of the possible consequences that his behavior, his decisions, could have upon his girls.* He does love them, but old habits die hard, *when they die at all,* and he isn't sure that he has the strength of character to resist the magnetism of *the yield.*

Book II - Yield

Teal

Renee, Earl, and Juanita

For the next three days, Renee does not go to work. Earl offers to stay home too, but she does not want him at home with her. For the first two of those days she is barely able to get out of bed, so debilitating is her pain. She lies in bed thinking: *if a husband who loves his wife can do what Earl did, what hope is there for any marriage to survive? If love doesn't assure fidelity, what does?*

On this, the third day, she is sitting at the kitchen table sipping hot tea. Her thoughts dance to and fro. Within her lonely spaciousness she feels naked; exposed, as if the fog of her depression will never lift. She gets these mental flashes of herself and Earl: *during the brief marriage ceremony exchanging their vows and rings; on their honeymoon in the Virgin Islands; haunting estate sales; deciding the exact placement of a piece of furniture; long mornings in bed when they both called in sick.* She can't seem to stop these thoughts, which is why she feels so exposed. *He knows how I feel. Felt!* She says to herself; *he knows what we have. Had! But it didn't stop him. It didn't even make him cautious. It's incomprehensible.* These thoughts penetrate her psyche as if they have a will of their own. She feels worn out by the fatigues of them, yet she feels incapable of halting them. For the past thirteen years, she's thought in twos: *we'll have to do this; we'll have to see about that; we'll let you know; we've decided we'll go to...* Now she is thinking: *I'll have to decide what I want to do.*

Book II - Yield

Teal

That evening, a Friday, as Earl comes through the door, he is carrying a huge bouquet of yellow roses, her favorite flower. She has gone back to bed. He places them on the bedside table and says, "I'm not going to say that I know how you feel, but I will say that you're not the only one in pain. If somehow I could convey to you how much it hurts me to know that I've caused you this sorrow, you'd understand why I'm saying this. Renee, I feel like I'm pleading for my life, for *our* life. I'm so sorry for what I've done. I know it's inexcusable, and I know it's unexplainable; I can't even explain it to myself. I'm asking you to forgive me. Can you? Will you give me a chance? Will you give *us* a chance to get beyond this and to work to recapture all the joy we've had? Please, I want the chance to make it up to you. It would be a shame to end all we've shared. God, I'm sorry."

At these words, tears anew fill Renee's eyes. She's too full of misery to speak. When she has composed herself a bit she says, "I really don't know if I can forgive you, Earl. If we had been experiencing some problems; if we had been argumentative or unpleasant with one another, maybe then I wouldn't be so clueless. But as it is, I have no idea why you slept with Juanita. I have no idea why you'd even allow yourself to be in a position where that could happen. I know there are women who would say *it's the testosterone*, but if it's that, what's the point in my forgiving you? You've still got that, and you're going to have it for a very long time, perhaps forever. So you tell me, what was the motivating force?"

Earl is silent for several moments. His eyes are filled with unshed tears. Finally he says, "I can't tell you why I did what I did. But I can tell you that it had nothing to do with my love for you. You know I love you. I don't think you'll deny that. It was something that just happened."

Now Renee says, "Earl, sex between two, adult people does not just happen. Decisions have to be made; people have to go to private places; people have to remove some of their clothing! People have to decide to have sex; it does not just happen, so don't tell me that it just happened!

"I don't know what else to say then. We certainly didn't plan it," he responds.

"Speak for yourself, Earl. You can't say whether she planned it or not! When she told you that her car wouldn't crank, did you get in it and try to start it for her? Did you check it out? When she said that she was hungry and asked you to stop for burgers, do you know for sure that that wasn't a ploy to delay your departure? When she offered you coffee that she said was already brewed...

"Hold it! Are you telling me that Juanita might've set out deliberately to get me into this situation?" Earl asks with incredulity.

Renee tells him that that is exactly what she is saying. She also tells him that grown women who don't want to, don't have to get pregnant. "You and I sleep together every night; we have for thirteen years. We have sex every night, and sometimes more than once a night. Have I ever been pregnant? Think about that!

For the first time, Earl begins to think about these things: *he wonders if her car was really disabled; if she really is a member of that spa; if she did set out to make this happen.* All of these things occupy his thoughts. He even recalls that playful kiss on the lips when he went to retrieve their coats that time at the Craig's house. Now he starts to get angry. He says to Rene, "You know, Renee, I didn't think"...

She interrupts with, "I know you didn't think; that's the problem, but that's no excuse. You're a grown man and you're expected to think!

"Wait a minute," he says, "hear me out. I didn't think an intelligent, attractive woman like Juanita would have to stoop that low."

"Maybe she didn't have to; maybe she chose to stoop that low. Maybe she thought that since you and I don't have kids, you'd be an easy target, that you'd jump at the chance to have a child of your own. Juanita doesn't travel in our circle; she knows nothing of our personal life. She probably doesn't know that you and I have chosen not to have children. Who knows what she thought?"

"You know, I think I'm beginning to know some of what she thought. She said something to me on the phone that time when she called here. You remember the time I told you about when you were in the shower and I answered the phone. She said something about the fact that you and I don't have kids. Renee asks exactly what Juanita said. "She said, (he pauses here to think, trying to remember her exact words), she had said to me earlier that her family is catholic, so abortion is no option for her. So I told her that divorce is no option for me because I love my wife. She just ignored that and said that since we don't have any kids, it shouldn't be too complicated for me to get a divorce. You know, I'm beginning to think a lot of this might have been contrived."

Renee doesn't respond to this last statement, but she is cognizant. She's had discussions about this plenty of times with other married women in their circle. There are some desperate women out there who, for whatever reasons, have not been able to meet and marry an eligible man or meet one in whom they are interested in marrying, and so they set out, deliberately, to entrap a married man. The more gullible the man, the easier it is to entrap him. Attractive, single women know this; they also know that the average man will offer to help them if they appear to be in distress; that it doesn't even occur to him that the situation has been contrived for his involvement. She says to herself, *but if they used the body part designed by God to do their thinking, they'd find themselves in a lot less difficulty!*

That Saturday when Earl goes to the spa for his workout, he stops by the desk and asks the attendant, "Do you have a woman named Juanita Spence who is a member here?"

"That name sounds familiar," the attendant says. "I think I signed her up for a trial membership myself not too long ago. In fact, I recall quite vividly because she hasn't been back since she signed up, and I recently tried to reach her to ask if there is a problem with the facility. We like to keep in touch with our customers, so we call the ones who don't come in regularly to workout."

"About how long ago was that? Can you remember?" Earl asks.

"Not exactly, but it was less that six months ago. I know that because it was during our last membership drive, which was less than six months ago."

Earl begins to get the picture. He has always thought of himself as a sophisticated man, so he can't believe he let himself be lead like a puppet; he can't believe he was so gullible. He can't believe that he's risked his life, and the life of his dear wife, simply because he didn't think. Well, he's thinking now, and he knows that *the yield* has probably cost him a once in a lifetime relationship!

Asa and Darryll

As Darryll is leaving the Officer's Club, he gets into his car and Vandross's *Power of Love* is playing softly on the radio. He reaches over and turns it off, not that he doesn't like it, *he does*, but whenever he hears it now, he is reminded of the time he spent with Asa in his bedroom.

He still hasn't called Asa, even though he's gotten several messages from his mom asking him to call home. He hasn't done that either, except for that one time when his mom told him about Asa's call to her; almost a week has gone by since that time. When Darryll arrives home, there is another message, this time from his father. He knows it's best not to ignore his father; he has a long history of doing what his father asks; he also knows that his father has called him only at his mother's urging. He decides to call Asa before returning his father's call.

"Hello, Asa, this is Darryll. How are you?" he asks.

"I'm okay, Asa says. "How are you?" *Maybe there's been some mixup,* Darryll says to himself; *maybe she really is okay.* But Asa dispels that notion in the next breath. She tells him, "I'm almost two months pregnant, Darryll. I've been trying to get in contact with you."

"My mom told me about that, just minutes ago. I've been very busy, so I haven't been checking my messages regularly, he says. But he's not in the habit of lying, and it shows.

Asa doesn't believe him, but she says nothing. As the silence lengthens, he says, "We need to talk about this. Are you free this weekend?" She tells him that she is. They discuss when and where they'll meet.

After they hang up, Darryll calls home. His mom answers the phone; she wants to know what has transpired between him and Asa. He tells her that he will see Asa this weekend, then he asks to speak to his father.

Right away his dad says, "What's this I hear about some girl being pregnant and trying to get in contact with you?"

Darryll and his dad have always been very close; he usually does not lie to his dad. He says, "Dad, Asa is a girl I met awhile back. She says she's carrying my child."

"Son, you've known since you were twelve how not to make a baby. I taught you better than that. I can't believe you're telling me that you had unprotected sex with a woman you hardly know," his dad replies.

"Who says I hardly know her, Dad?" Darryll asks.

"Asa is a girl I met awhile back, is what you said. That means you hardly knew her. Besides, if you'd known her for any length of time, chances are good I'd already know her too. Does that answer your question?" he asks.

Darryll does not respond to this, but he recognizes that it is entirely true. In fact, he has repeatedly berated himself for his moments of weakness, as he thinks of the time he spent in his room with Asa. He has thought often of late of what his dad said to him when he was only twelve about how a moment of weakness could change the course of a person's life, and how, at that time, he hadn't a clue what that meant. *Well, he knows now*!

That weekend when he and Asa meet, his first thought is: *God, I'd forgotten how beautiful she is.* There is no visible evidence of the pregnancy, *but maybe her slender face does appear a bit fuller,* he thinks.

He can't take his eyes away from her face. He just keeps staring. When she appears a little uneasy by this close scrutiny he says, "I apologize for staring, but I'd forgotten how beautiful you are." He hadn't meant to say that; it just came out, spontaneously. He has the transitory thought that *in Asa's presence he does things that he would not ordinarily do; he says things that he does not intend to say.*

"How do you know that you're pregnant with my child?" he asks. For the second time, within minutes, he has said something which he has not meant to say. Certainly he wants to know the answer to that question, but he had not meant to ask her. He had meant to engage her in conversation and to draw his own conclusions from what she had to say. He is on the brink of an apology, but before he can make it Asa says, "I know I'm pregnant because I've had a pregnancy test, two in fact; both were positive. I know it's your child because I've never been intimate with anyone else. Does that tell you what you want to know?" she asks.

He ignores her question and says, "What do you want to do?"

Asa tells him that it's not about what she wants to do. "If it were about that," she says, "there would have been no need to contact you. I would have just had an abortion, or carried the baby full-term and then given birth. But because of my own childhood, I feel that the decision to give birth shouldn't be about what a woman does or does not want, nor should it be about what a man does or does not want, especially after the pregnancy is a fact.

Darryll ponders this. To a large extent, he feels likewise. His respect for Asa has risen as he listened to her. *There's more here than what meets the eye,* he says to himself. Then he says to her, "Tell me about your childhood." She tells him about the first time she realized her mother was an alcoholic; about the brief periods of happiness when her mother was *on the wagon*. She shares with him the time when she had the lead in the sixth grade play, and was afraid that her mother wouldn't show up to see her perform, and also afraid that she would show up drunk and embarrass her. When she still doesn't mention her father he says, "What about your dad?"

"What about him?" she asks.

"Does he try to get her to stop drinking? Does he drink too?" Darryll wants to know.

"I never knew my father; I've never met him. My mother always said that he knew where to find us if he wanted us, but I guess he didn't want us; he never found us, never came for us. I used to daydream about him coming to rescue me." She is silent now; for a long moment each is quiet, pensive.

"Then I guess we'll have to get married," Darryll says. He hadn't meant to say that, although he was thinking it, but somehow saying it makes it real for him, makes him realize that that is exactly what he wants to do. He can feel his lips forming a smile, seemingly of their own volition.

"How're your parents going to feel about this?" Asa asks.

"They probably won't like the idea, especially my mom, but I'm a grown man; I make my own decisions. Come on, we might as well go tell them now. There's no point in delaying the inevitable," he says.

"Why don't you go tell them; give them a chance to get used to the idea before introducing me to them?" she suggests.

Darryll does not say so, but he knows they will try to talk him out of it if he goes alone, and he has decided that he wants to marry her. He wants her with him when he tells them, so he says, "I think we should do it together. We got ourselves into this together, didn't we?"

In the living room at his parents' home, Darryll introduces the three of them and says, "We've decided to get married." His dad is looking at Asa. She reminds him of someone he knows, or once knew. *She looks so familiar,* he says to himself. His mom is thinking, *at least she's pretty. But what else is she? My son is a prize; I'm not handing him over to just anyone who comes aknockin'.*

His mom says, "Tell us about yourself, Young Lady? Where are you from? Where did you attend school?"

Asa tells her, "I grew up right here in the Chicago area. I'm now in the army. I joined the army to earn money for college." During all of this, Darwin, Darryll's dad, is quiet, studying Asa, trying to place that face. Suddenly it hits him! *She looks just like Amelia, their daughter; they look enough alike to be sisters, twins even.*

Now he begins to think about that period, *almost twenty years ago now, when he and Mamie were separated for about six months. During that time, he had slept with a woman. Once. He had used a condom, but it had ruptured. Never before had anything like that ever happened to him; it was traumatic. He'll never forget that time because it was around the same time period when he first learned about the AIDS virus. For months afterwards it was all he could think of. He imagined every little pain, every itch, every insect bite, the beginning of the end. But nothing happened, so eventually he felt okay about it. When he and Mamie reconciled, he even told her about it, believing it was the right thing to do. He explained that he didn't think he'd been infected, but he couldn't be sure about an unwanted or unplanned*

Book II - Yield

Teal

pregnancy. Mamie had agonized about it for days, but had finally decided to reconcile. They already had a five-year-old son, Darryll, who was crazy about his father. Darryll and his dad were close, even then. She knew he needed his father, and family was important to her; she knew its value. Shortly after the reconciliation, Mamie got pregnant with Amelia, who is now eighteen. Asa is nineteen. *I wonder how old she is,* Darwin is thinking.

When Asa and Darryll leave, Darwin confides his suspicions to Mamie. She tells him, "Probably not. There are millions of people here. The chance of something that bizarre happening are infinitesimal." But still, both of them are afraid, though neither shares this fear with the other one. Both are also *wondering how one would go about confirming something like that without arousing undue, and probably unnecessary, suspicions in others.*

Mamie has Asa's phone number. *Maybe I should call her,* she says to herself. *Maybe I can find out who she is. I'll bet anything she knows her father. It can't be Darwin; it just can't be.*

Mamie has been able to think of nothing else for more than a week now. She's been debating with herself. Before she can change her mind, she gets up and dials Asa's phone number; she gets the answering machine. She hangs up without leaving a message and dials Darryll's number. Again she gets the answering machine. "I hate these damned machines! she says aloud to the empty room, slamming down the phone.

Meanwhile, Darryll and Asa are making plans. They plan to get married the following weekend. Darryll's dad has asked him not to make any hasty decisions, to talk with him first before making any final plans. He has promised his dad that he will do this. He calls his dad and says, "Dad,

Asa and I have decided, *definitely*, to be married this next weekend. We don't want any fuss; we'll just go to the courthouse before it closes on Friday evening."

"Son," Darwin says, "you can't do that. You have family who has always expected to be with you when you got married. You have people who love you, and I'm sure Asa has parents who expect the same of her. What about them? What about us? How would you like it if Amelia sneaked off to the courthouse and married without your knowledge; without your presence?"

Darryll tells him that he isn't sneaking off. "If I were sneaking off, would we be having this conversation?" he asks. "Would I be telling you what our plans are?"

"Let your mother know your plans; call her. Give her a chance to at least plan a small reception for the two of you," Darwin advises.

But what his dad is really hoping is that Mamie Lee will be able to convince Darryll to wait. He wants time to ascertain that Asa is not Darryll's and Amelia's half sister. He knows that he should tell Darryll this, but he cannot. Neither of his children knows anything about that brief period when he and Mamie were separated. Amelia wasn't even born when it happened. Darwin has instilled in his children the importance of family. He cannot bring himself to tell Darryll that he left him and his mother once. He is ashamed of it, and he doesn't want to have to explain about that period. He wants to forget it it, and in fact, he almost had.

Darryll does not want to call his mother. He didn't really want to call his dad, but he had promised that he would, and so he did. He knows that his mother will try to talk him out of marrying Asa, and he has made up his mind to do so.

Meanwhile, Asa has gone home to tell her mother of the approaching nuptials. When she tells her, her mother asks, "Who's the lucky guy?"

"His name is Darryll Crenshaw," Asa says.

"Crenshaw? That's your father's name," Rose Marie finally shares with her. *Never before has she volunteered anything about her father, and even when pressed, her responses to Asa's long ago questions never ever revealed his name.*

"What did you say?" Asa asks, surprised at this revelation.

"I said Crenshaw is your father's last name," she says again.

Now Asa asks why she always calls herself Asa Masden if her father's last name is Crenshaw. Rose Marie tells her, "Masden is my maiden name, and since your father and I didn't ever even talk about getting married, I didn't put his name on your birth certificate. I just always thought of you as mine, as a Masden, and that's what I called you." As she is saying this, Asa is thinking: *there must be thousands of people right here in this area with the last name of Crenshaw. It's not an unusual name. All of them can't be related.*

Later that evening when Darryll calls, she tells him about the conversation she had with her mother. "That is weird," he says, *but he doesn't give any thought to the idea that it's likely that they're related.*

The following day when Darryll reluctantly calls his mother, she urges him to wait for a couple of weeks. "Asa's already pregnant, so what's the rush?" she asks. "If you two will wait a couple of weeks or so, I'm willing to plan a wedding and reception for you. I'll invite both families and a few close friends; do things the right way. I'm sure her mother and father would like to see their daughter come down the aisle. A daughter should be on her father's arm on her wedding day, Darryll. You know that," she says.

Darryll tells her that Asa doesn't know her father, and that her mother is ill and will not be able to attend the ceremony. He tells her that they don't want a wedding, but they've agreed to a small reception. "What do you mean, she doesn't know her father?" Mamie inquires. "She must know something about him. What's his name?" she asks.

"I know this is odd, but his name is Crenshaw," he says.

"Is Crenshaw his first or last name?" she asks.

"It's his last name," he says.

"Then what's his first name?" she wants to know.

"I don't know, Mother. What difference does it make what his first or last name is? The significant point is that he is not a part of her life and never has been. I should think that's all we need to know," he concludes.

But that is not all they need to know. *They need to know if he has, by some bizarre twist of fate, met and made love to his own stepsister. They need to know if it is his stepsister who is expecting his child. They need to know if they should advise Asa to have an abortion. They need to know if they should tell him that he can't possibly marry Asa, that she is his half sister.*

When Mamie hangs up, she calls Darwin into the kitchen and pours each of them a cup of coffee. As they sit drinking the coffee she says, "Darwin, we're going to have to get to the bottom of this. Like you, I had decided that it couldn't be, it was just too improbable, almost inconceivable. But it's none of these things." Now she relates the conversation she just had with Darryll, ending with, "Do you remember this woman's last name? Have you any idea where now she lives?"

Darwin tells her that the woman's name was Rosie *something*, but that he has no idea where she now lives. "I've had no contact with her since that one time over twenty years ago. I don't think I'd even recognize her if she walked into this room."

"In that case," Mamie says, "we have no choice but to call Darryll and share our suspicions with him. We can't just do nothing and hope the problem will solve itself. That's irresponsible and I'll not be a party to it."

Darwin tells Mamie that he taught Darryll to be responsible; that not a week went by during his teen years that he did not talk to him about how being sexually irresponsible could change the course of a young man's life forever. "If I have to tell him about that long ago period, what is he going to think of me? If I'm forced to share that with him, how will he feel then about all of those man-to-man talks? *Damn! I wish I'd taken my own advice.*"

"We both wish that, but this wishing business is preposterous at this point. We've got to decide on a course of action, and follow it!" Mamie says.

For several minutes, both are quiet, introspective. The ringing phone startles them. It is Darryll. "There's been an accident," he says. "I'm fine, but Asa has been injured; she's being taken to the hospital. I'll call you from there as soon as I know her condition."

"What happened?" Mamie asks. But the line is already dead; Darryll has hung up. They don't even know to which hospital Asa's been taken; he didn't think to say.

Book II - Yield

"What did he say?" Darwin asks. She tells him the little she knows about the accident; that Darryll isn't hurt; that Asa has been injured.

Later that night Darryll calls from the hospital. Asa is okay, *but she has lost the baby.* He tells them that the accident happened when a man ran a red light and hit the rental car which Darryll was driving. "He was traveling around sixty miles an hour and almost demolished Asa's side of the car. It's a miracle we weren't killed, or badly injured. You should see the car. They had to cut us out," he says.

Neither voices it, but both are relieved. They both know, without further investigation, that Asa is indeed who they had hoped she would not turn out to be. But there are just too many coincidences for them to conclude anything else. They both realize precisely what *the yield* could have netted.

To the Reader

The author wishes to acknowledge her awareness of the fact that all people, of all races, both men and women, do wrong. The scenarios contained herein simply illustrate a mere fraction of the ways some Black men involve themselves in situations and circumstances which assist in the disintegration and destruction of the Black family. There are countless others, far too many to be included in any single book.

I urge the Black man to stop living double lives. He needs to stop trying to hang onto his family on the one hand and lead the life of a single gigolo on the other. He needs to come to grips with the reality that only he can provide his children the opportunity to experience, firsthand, the interactions between their happily married parents. Only he can afford his children the chance to experience what it is like to see their parents face problems and work through them. He needs to accept as part of his reality that the example he sets for his son during his son's formative years will be the one that his son is most likely to follow. He needs to love his children enough to make whatever sacrifices that must be made in order to assure that their home environment is one that fosters a positive self-concept and an appreciation of what it means to be loved sacrificially.

The Black man must willingly assume the responsibility for making provisions for his children, and the provisions that he makes must be more than merely monetary. Of course it takes money to provide for his children, but money is not the *end all* that some Black men seem to believe it to be. Money cannot get up through the night to tend a sick baby. Money cannot create the bonding between a man and his children that only his presence can foster. The Black man must accept this reality if he has any hope of rescuing his children from the drug, gang and low-achieving abyss into which too many of them have fallen prey.

Some Black men can still be heard to complain about how, during slavery, the white man tore the Black man from the bosom of his family, or tore his family from his bosom. Well, it's not the white man who is doing the tearing now! It is the Black man who is tearing and ripping to shreds the strong fibers of which the Black family is woven, the potent fibers that the institution of slavery was unable to sever. It is going to take the Black man's assistance, willing presence and his enthusiastic family involvement to reweave these fibers into the happy, healthy, complete and thriving Black family.

The Yield

Fathers,
The Yield is not worth it.
Your children are crying.
Your children are dying.
Fathers,
The yield is not worth it.

Fathers,
Your children are lonely.
They miss the love you can give.
Please, fathers, abandon the yield.
Your children need the love you should give!

Fathers, your sons will to emulate you.
They see and will mimic all that you do.
Give them a model; give them a guide.
In your behavior, don't have to hide!

Fathers,
Abandon the women; the wine.
Loving one woman forever is fine!
Nourish your sons and daughters.
Give them your prime time!

Fathers,
The yield is not worth it.
What can you possibly yield
That is worth the love you get when you give?
Fathers,
The yield is not worth it!

Epilogue

To the beautiful, Black men who have kept the commitments that they have made and have made the inevitable sacrifices to assure their continuous roles in the lives of their families, their loved ones, I salute them. They know who they are and their loved ones know who they are. *Would that the whole world could know who they are!*

Please know that this book was not written to imply that there is no such being as the *loving, moral* and *open Black man. There is!* This book was not written to imply that *only* the Black man involves himself in situations and circumstances such as the ones spotlighted herein. *That is certainly untrue!*
There are far too many Black men, however, who repeatedly involve themselves in these kinds of situations, and by so doing they are contributing to the delinquency, the unhappiness and the diminishing sense of self-worth of their own children. Further, they are lessening their children's chances of living happy, successful and productive lives. They are instrumental in the *destruction of the Black family. These men know who they are, and their loved ones know who they are.*

It is my prayer that these men will not continue to erode the strong fibers that comprise the beautiful, healthy and thriving Black family. This book is an appeal to them. They can save the Black family. What will they do? It's up to them!

Book II - Yield

Teal

Ordering Information

To order copies of this book, or any of the following publications, send your request to: Joyce W. Teal
　　　　　8629 Forest Green Dr.
　　　　　Dallas, TX 75243

Publications available at this time include:

Publication
- ☐ *It's O.K. To Be Different*　　1-57502-238-9　　$6.99
- ☐ *The Point System*　　1-56763-399-4　　$8.95
- ☐ *Sister, It's Not Okay*　　0-9660215-1-7　　$10.00
- ☐ *The Yield*　　0-9660215-3-3　　$10.00

To order, visit **Black Images** or **Jokae's s Books in Dallas, TX**, **Barnes & Nobles** or **Waldenbooks** nationwide, or send the cost of the book(s) of your choice. Include $2.50 for shipping and handling charges**,** to the address above. Be sure to include your:

Name _____

Address_____

_____

Please include your correct **zip code!**